D0483757

wolf land

Carter Niemeyer

Published by BottleFly Press

Also by Carter Niemeyer

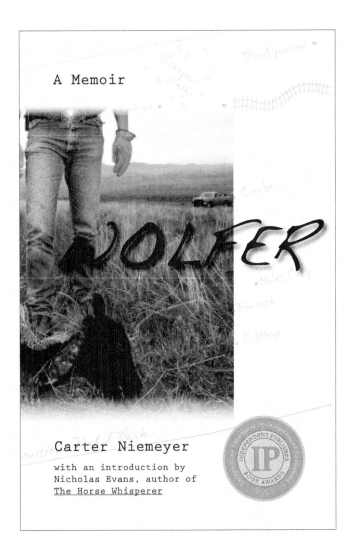

A Memoir

WOLFER

Carter Niemeyer

with an introduction by
Nicholas Evans, author of
The Horse Whisperer

Wolf Land

Edited by Jenny Niemeyer and Dee Lane
Cover and interior designed by Beth Fischer
Maps copyright © Jenny Niemeyer

"Don't Think Twice, It's All Right"
The Freewheelin' Bob Dylan, Oct. 15, 1962.
Used with permission, Bob Dylan Music Co.

OR-7 cartoon © Oregonian Publishing Co.,
Reprinted with permission

This is a work of non-fiction. All of the events actually
happened. Some names and identifying details have been
changed or omitted to protect the privacy of individuals.
Nothing is intended or should be interpreted as expressing or
representing the views of the United States government or
other government agencies or departments.

Library of Congress Cataloging-in-Publication Data
Niemeyer, Carter, 1947 –
1. Nature 2. Biography
2015918420
ISBN 978-0-9848113-2-8
Also available in Kindle edition, ISBN 978-0-9848113-3-5

Printed in the United States of America

10 9 8 7 6 5 4 3 2 1

For my parents, Slats and Opal, who never went west.

"You're the reason I'm trav'lin' on
Don't think twice, it's all right."

- Bob Dylan

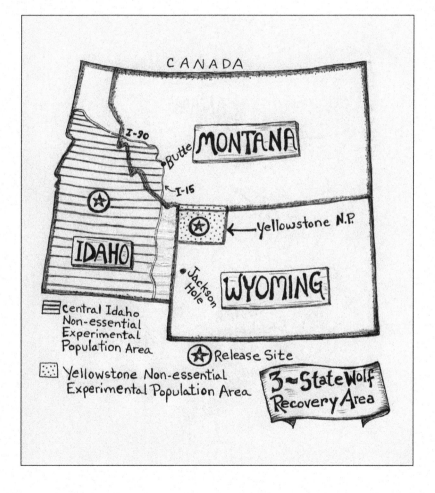

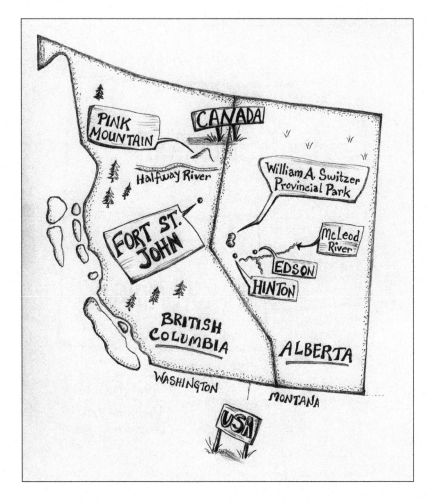

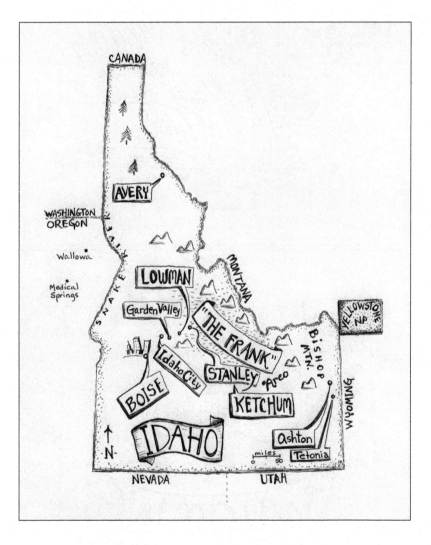

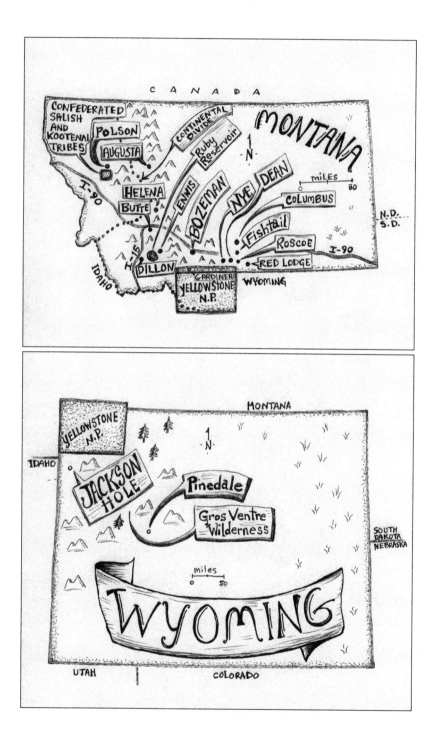

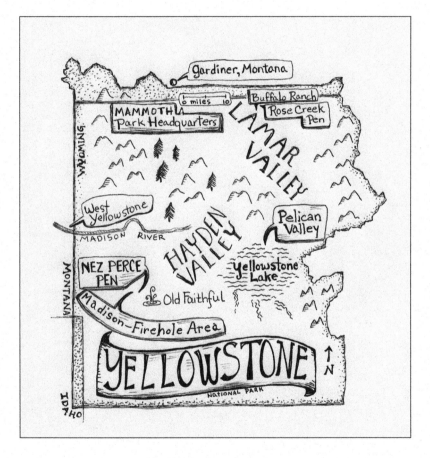

Gardiner, Montana

0 miles 10

MAMMOTH
Park Headquarters

Buffalo Ranch
Rose Creek
Pen

WYOMING

LAMAR VALLEY

West Yellowstone

MADISON RIVER

HAYDEN VALLEY

Pelican Valley

Yellowstone Lake

NEZ PERCE PEN

MONTANA

Old Faithful

Madison-Firehole Area

YELLOWSTONE
NATIONAL PARK

↑N

IDAHO

Sunrise at wolf camp in Idaho.
(Photo by Carter Niemeyer)

Ghosts in Bear Valley

In late August the forest roads are dry as flour, even after the overnight dew has settled and gathered in drops on my dirty windshield. Early is best. So early that the sky is barely gray, and only an occasional robin echoes down some canyon. We rub sleep from our eyes. Still wearing our dusty clothes from yesterday, we unzip the tent flaps, lace our boots, take a pee. Start the truck now. Food can wait.

We head out without talking much, my wife, Jenny and I, anticipating the wolves. We found good signs of them yesterday on the edge of the central Idaho wilderness in a place called Bear Valley. And in that first light of day when I know where the wolves are, I feel excited like I'm still a little kid.

We drive on, slowly. We pass the U.S. Forest Service check-in station. No one there – too early. The road narrows and gets bumpier. I slow more, trying to rattle as little as possible, and send up the very smallest cloud of dust. The dirt road cuts to the edge of an island of lodgepole pines. Ahead of us is Ayers Meadows. I coast to a stop, roll down the windows, shut off the engine and pull the key halfway out to silence the buzzer. The sudden, fat silence makes me realize yet again how much noise humans make – and the silly idea that we can be sneaky in a place like this.

The meadow is vast and wrapped in long blanket of fog. So we sit. I swig some water from yesterday. Jenny finds a can of peanuts. Then – shh. We stop chewing.

A single, lonesome sound floats into our open windows. A wolf. Maybe a half mile away, but right in front of us – the Bear Valley pack.

Minutes later, I see movement in the trees to my left. Two men in camo climb out of the brush and start up the road toward us, coming up alongside the truck.

"Did you hear those wolves?" one whispers. Their faces are smeared with brown paint. Each is bundled in high-end hunting gear and has a bow slung over one shoulder – archery hunters at work on one of the first days of the season.

"I was sitting out there next to a tree before daylight and that fog hadn't moved in yet," one says, pointing at the valley, barely able to hold his voice at a whisper. "I could see all these wolves in front of me. I took some video of them. Man, what a cool sight."

"I've never been this close to wolves before," the other hunter says, almost smiling. "They got a dead elk out there, I think."

We agree. Pretty cool. Then they move on.

Jenny and I sit in silence. The howling sounds like dozens of wolves. Maybe that's how they intimidate – by making themselves seem to be more than just a few. The eerie moans bounce off the hills and return again, making it hard to judge distance. How far from us are they? A quarter mile? We step out of the truck and leave the doors ajar, trying to stay quiet. Jenny flips her camera to video mode and records the ghosts before us. We hear the echoes of an occasional skirmish among the wolves, but see only faint movement in the distance.

Soon the howls change to deep, rhythmic barks. We're busted, or else those bow hunters got too close. You can't get away with being near wolves without them hearing or smelling you. When they're irritated or upset, they howl-bark. We wait and, as the valley lightens and the fog lifts slightly, we can see small shadows moving back and forth, lying down, standing, moving again. Jenny looks through the binoculars and counts. Fourteen.

My radio telemetry receiver doesn't pick up the one collar I know is in this group. Earlier in the week, a retired couple volunteering as firewatchers at one of the Forest Service campgrounds reported seeing a pack of fifteen wolves. I wasn't ready to believe that. People get excited and overestimate things. But now, with the wolves in front of us, I make a mental note to visit those folks again to let them know they were right, and thank them. I can always use a reliable source.

The wolves move around in the veil of white, focused mostly on a dark bump in the middle of the meadow – the elk carcass, presumably. Big wolves and smaller wolves. Ravens swarm, waiting for a turn. We watch for an hour or so, occasionally turning on the telemetry receiver to check for the radio-collared wolf. It's not there. Soon the valley goes quiet. The wolves steal away, disappearing one by one into the steep country to the east, away from people like us who want to pry into their lives.

Bear Valley lies at the edge of "The Frank," the 2.3-million acre federal Frank Church-River of No Return Wilderness in central Idaho. As the crow flies, Bear Valley is 20 miles north of Lowman, a tiny hamlet with little more than a gas pump, a café, and a church. For decades, Bear Valley's lush meadows and wildflowers were used as cattle feed, but today it's one of a handful of wild places that cows and sheep don't invade. It wasn't wolves or some other charismatic megafauna that did it, but salmon, which need clean streams. A fish kicked the cows out of Bear Valley. Somehow that's funny to me. When I think of all the ranchers who told me wolves would put them out of business, I think of this place.

But Bear Valley – big, wild, free of livestock and full of game
– can, by its very isolated nature, be a threat to wolves. Remote
areas allow people to do their deeds in immense privacy, so that
people who might object are unaware. Some of the deeds that
resulted in dead wolves were performed by state or federal wildlife agencies. In other cases, private citizens have gone out of
their way, and even spent a fair amount of money, to get into
the backcountry with the sole purpose of poisoning wolves. The
collateral damage to vultures, eagles, bears and anything else
that ate their tainted meat was acceptable. Why some people do
such things is hard to guess, other than the most obvious reason:
fear. But if wolves can't live in the wilderness, where can they
live?

Wolves had been seen here and there in the remote areas
of Idaho before federal reintroduction in the mid-1990s, but
none appeared to stay, and certainly they weren't established
and breeding. In 1991, one of the first wolves to reappear in the
state in many decades was killed near Bear Valley. News stories,
always on the front page, recounted how the 90-pound female
wolf had been kicked to death by another animal. Later, law
enforcement officials announced that poison had killed it. The
wolf probably took only a few steps before it was dead from the
insecticide Furadan, which had been added to a chunk of meat.
It was effective, but not an approved use of the chemical. The
feds stalled before telling anyone about it, hoping the culprit
would get sloppy and brag about it to the wrong stranger.

Furadan is a trade name for carbofuran, which is essentially
a neurotoxin, and can be deadly to most creatures – including
humans. In the mid-1970s, when I first went to work as a
federal trapper, I had heard of the insecticide being put in livestock carcasses in Montana to kill coyotes, which of course also
killed eagles, hawks, skunks and anything else that consumed
the treated meat. Back then, it was scattered liberally around
Montana, without much regard to secondary poisonings. The
volatile stuff even killed scavengers that ate the carcass of the

predator that consumed the poison. I heard stories about rings of dead insects around animal carcasses that had been illegally treated with Furadan. Federal wildlife agents told me not to handle any creature that I suspected had been poisoned. The airborne fumes of Furadan inside of a car sickened one federal agent who picked up and bagged an eagle that had been illegally poisoned with the insecticide. He said he put the carcass in the back of his SUV, but it was still in the passenger compartment. Always put carcasses in the back of your pickup, agents told me. I thought about that. I'd made plenty of U-turns for decent looking carcasses. Could be nice fur if it was winter and the carcass hadn't been run over too many times, or if it had, bait for wolf trapping. I wondered about the intelligence of a person who would endanger his own health by handling such chemicals in ways they weren't intended. In the end it was mostly dogs, not wolves that were killed by ingesting such substances.

The poisoning death of that wolf set off searches for more of the animals in the Idaho wilderness. Wolves, mostly extinct in the lower 48 states since the early part of the 20th century, had been heading south a few at a time from Canada, following the Continental Divide into Montana and Idaho. They'd done it without being noticed, for the most part. Still, the experts agreed: Wolf persecution had never stopped. Whether it was guns, traps, snares or poison, people picked off every wolf like it was some kind of arcade game. A few got established in the state, but they were isolated from each other, and a long way apart. The government generated reams of paperwork and held dozens of public hearings before scientists concluded that reintroducing many wolves at once was the only way to let them get a foothold. It wasn't going to happen with a few coming in here and there because they didn't appear to be finding each other. In 1995 and 1996, I worked on the project, and it changed the course of my life.

We took wolves from two similar elk systems in Canada and released them in the only areas we could find that met three requirements: plenty of elk, few people, and no livestock. The places were Yellowstone National Park and two locations in Idaho: Corn Creek and Dagger Falls, both in The Frank, not far from Bear Valley. In total, 66 wolves were turned loose, 31 in Yellowstone, and 35 of them right out of their crates and into the icy Idaho wilderness – a place where, despite all of the people who would like to see them die trying, the wolves would have no problem getting re-established.

When I drove to Canada on a snowy November day in 1994, I thought I was going to have a great time, help out a little with the wolf move and come home, where everything would be just like I had left it. Instead, I found myself deeper and deeper in the wolf issue, knowing more about the politics of this creature than I ever cared to. I'd fallen into wolf work almost ten years earlier without even realizing it. It wasn't sudden, but gradual. A problem here, then there. A wolf or two showed up, then four or five.

A lot of what has happened with wolves in the twenty years since reintroduction has not been happy. The main purpose of the Endangered Species Act is to protect the species, not individual animals. While the law makes killing an endangered animal a crime, there are all sorts of loopholes. When all was said and done, we killed a wolf for every cow a wolf killed. In the beginning, we didn't know how the wolves would do, and every individual mattered. When we realized how prolific and resilient they were, we just killed them, even when the reason was flimsy. As a federal trapper and later a wolf manager, I drove almost a million miles across Montana, Idaho and Wyoming in my government truck, talking to people, setting traps, soothing nerves. Nobody much wanted to go deal with the rural folks who experienced wolves up close, but I discovered that I was good at it. Maybe it was because I let them do most of the talking. I did what I could to get people to tolerate this new varmint on the landscape. It's just a wolf. The world is not ending. At first I was thrilled to get to handle a wolf, and was honored to have them in my care. Later I just thought, you poor bastard. You're going to end up dead. Some did and some didn't. There were no guarantees and no way to know what would come next.

Since reintroduction, wolves have expanded their range more than 400 miles farther south than any of us figured, so they've done pretty well, despite it all. It's people who are a mess and probably always will be when it comes to this creature. While we wring our hands and create bureaucracy to deal with wolves – and our reaction to them – the wolves are out there, ignoring us, living their lives, traveling great distances to find new ground, being more resilient than we will ever be.

I'll never forget what rancher Betty Baker asked on the day before I had to kill an entire pack of wolves in Idaho for eating calves: "If all you're going to do is kill them, why did you bring them back?" I've never heard a satisfactory answer, and sometimes I wonder about it myself. But on that foggy morning when Jenny and I listened to the wolves howl in Bear Valley, I think I knew.

Beginnings: The Rose Creek Wolves

I held a piece of paper in one hand and dialed the phone in my motel room with the other. Trapper Wade Berry answered. He was the first person on my list.

"So, you're one of the only guys snaring wolves this winter?" I asked after a few pleasantries. I figured I might as well jump right into it.

"Nah, there are others," Wade said. He didn't sound very enthusiastic.

Wade was the quintessential Canadian fur trapper. He and his wife lived in a cabin in the woods 25 miles outside of Hinton, Alberta. He built his cabin and most of the furniture in it. Wade made money killing fur-bearing animals, wolves mostly, and selling them to the fur market, which in turn sold them world-wide to garment manufacturers and taxidermists. Wolves have virtually no protection in Canada and can be hunted or trapped or snared almost year-round. The animals tolerated the pressure; there always seemed to be plenty of them around. That was good for people like Wade, who depended on them for a living. It wasn't an easy job or lifestyle given the cold winters. Like other fur trappers, he mostly snared his prey rather than trapped them because traps don't work well in wet or snowy weather. He was up early and out late, driving, picking up his kill, skinning, and re-setting snares. He was grubby most of the time, but it's what he loved and he was damn good at it. I'd known Wade a very short while, a few days maybe, when his trapping partner challenged me to a wolf-skinning contest on Wade's living room carpet. They both were pretty sure I was just a bureaucrat, so I slung a dead, black wolf over one leg and went to it, with the sole intention of gaining Wade's trust. By the time I'd won that impromptu wager, the carpet was ruined, I was seeing double from too much chokecherry wine, and I'd cut my thumb good and deep. But Wade and I had bonded.

As a trapper myself, I felt like I was the only member of our American team who understood these guys. Good thing, because time was wasting. I was in Alberta, Canada, stationed in Hinton, a mill town of about 10,000 surrounded by forest, to help piece together Northern Rockies wolf reintroduction. I fell into this situation by accident, coming to Montana from Iowa in 1973, shortly after I graduated from Iowa State University. I had earned a master's degree, but I took a job trapping rabid skunks because it sounded exotic, and because I loved trapping. I'd never been to the West. From there, I went into coyote control for the feds, and once wolves started wandering in from Canada, I became a wolf trapper because I was the guy to deal with the livestock they might kill. That experience got me onto the reintroduction team. It sounded exciting, and I was eager to help. I made the drive north from my home in Helena in a snowstorm that got worse with every passing hour. Once there, it took me about a day to figure out that legwork that needed to precede wolf captures seemed to have fizzled, which was why I was now on the phone in my motel room. I thought I was there to help; instead I'd suddenly received a field promotion to unofficial project leader.

It was a matter of perfect timing that the reintroduction of wolves back into America's Northern Rockies ever happened. The economy was booming and government agencies were pretty well funded. An aggressive group of advocates clamored for it, and politicians made it happen. Part of the reason Western politicians could swallow it was that reintroduction came with a side benefit: controlling problem wolves. The animals were migrating from Canada anyway, but without special management under the Endangered Species Act, they couldn't be killed or moved or even touched. It was a fine bit of bargaining.

The wolves we planned on capturing weren't that far from Yellowstone or Idaho. The idea of moving wolves south had been brewing for at least a decade before it actually happened in two installments in 1995 and 1996. None of us realized how tough these animals really were, or how difficult it would be for people from all walks of life to think differently about them. They're not evil, and they're not magical. They're animals, and in the years to come it would be my greatest wish that we could just leave them alone.

But at the moment, the crucial job was to find the guys who could find us wolves. Things needed to happen, said Ed Bangs, the Northern Rockies wolf reintroduction project leader, back in Helena. Everybody back in the states was under the impression that we would just swoop in and get the wolves and be done with it. But there were those pesky details. Things had fallen apart when it came to contracts between the trappers and the U.S. government. Paperwork that was supposed to be signed hadn't been. No one had really even talked to most of the trappers who were running regular snare lines and who were supposed to supply us with live wolves. The trappers were pissed off by the time I arrived, and in the meantime, wolves that could have been collected for reintroduction were dying in snares.

The slip of paper in my hand didn't match what Wade was telling me. He and another fellow, George Kelly, were the only Hinton trappers on my list who had signed contracts with the U.S. government. They were the only ones who had changed their routines and stopped killing wolves on their productive snare lines. They had clamped metal stops onto their snare cables, which would prevent the snare from tightening down on the wolf's neck, suffocating it.

The whole of Alberta was divided into registered trap lines, so we couldn't just go get wolves wherever we desired. We were counting on local trappers to help, but most of them seemed either unaware or disinterested in America's little reintroduction project. Wade and George were the exceptions, and my saviors. At least I hoped they were.

"Well, Wade, I could sure use your help finding those fellas and getting us some live wolves."

Wade knew everyone who called himself a trapper and he assured me he could deliver. He warned me though.

"If I call you in the middle of the night, you better get your ass up here," he said, and then gave me details on his friend Rick Stelter, who had snare lines in the woods near Edson. It was an hour's drive east from where I stood. Wade didn't have to explain his attitude. He and his trapper friends were done with bullshit promises tossed around by Americans.

I hung up, an inch closer to having live wolves. I lifted the receiver again and dialed Ed Bangs in Helena. He seemed relieved to hear something was happening. If he hadn't led with his chin, nothing would have gotten done on the Canadian end during reintroduction. "Do whatever you need to, Carter. We need things happening there." He meant it, and spent all of his time fighting off politicians and bureaucrats with his whip and chair, as he liked to put it.

We worked well together, even though we couldn't have been less alike in regular life. He goes to plays and concerts; I spell culture with a "k." Once, in a group of people, he and others wondered about what kind of bat was circling overhead in the quiet dusk of the day. You want to know? I asked. I retrieved my shotgun and blasted the little varmint out of the sky. All of them, Ed included, were appalled, looking with open mouths at the little bat that lay dead at their feet. We were just different kinds of people, even though now I feel bad for the bat.

I wanted Ed's explicit permission to get wolves from trappers who hadn't yet signed on the dotted line, and he explained how to go about getting through federal red tape. I knew if the trappers bothered with all of the hassle of saving wolves, they'd want to be paid pronto, and that was the carrot I was going to use. Each live wolf was worth $2,000, a hell of a lot more than they were getting for a pelt stretched on a board. I needed more than just Wade and George involved, though. More trappers meant faster results. We'd already been set up for a week at nearby William A. Switzer Provincial Park with our kennels, biologists, veterinarians and volunteers. We had media galore. We needed wolves.

A few days later, on December 3, 1994, Rick Stelter checked the snares he'd set. They hung near the McLeod River, innocent as twigs, across animal trails. He had five wolves – a family, most likely. Three were dead, while two still struggled. In the late afternoon, my phone rang.

"Rick's got a couple. Should we save them for you?" Wade said.

I pulled out of the parking lot at the Tara Vista motel as fast as I could gather my gear. Wade gave me directions to Edson and said that Rick would be parked at a highway turnoff on the west edge of town. I asked LuRay Parker, staff photographer for Wyoming Wildlife magazine, and veterinarians Dr. Mark Johnson and Dr. Janet Jones to follow in another truck. We made the 60-mile journey as it was getting dark. The sky and everything around us was black by the time we slowly worked our way through 10 miles of narrow, snow-packed trails called seismic lines. Seismographers had created the trails to study under-ground geology in the event the area contained coal or oil. The region was laced with them, and trappers – and wolves – gave them regular use.

As soon as we stepped out of our warm trucks, I heard brush cracking. We flipped on our headlamps and flashlights and made our way through a grove of skinny aspens and tangled brush. Our lights hit upon a frozen contorted wolf carcass, one of the victims of Rick's successful snare line. We passed a second dead wolf, then a third, each in bizarre configurations, their eyes fixed on nothing, like tiny, still mirrors. The snow around their twisted bodies was churned with dirt, betraying the last struggle of their short lives. Up ahead, I could hear an animal thrashing fero-ciously, snapping tree limbs.

Our lights picked up the glow of eyes and in a few more steps we could see a black wolf lying with its head down, watching us. It looked like a pup of the year, maybe eight months old, judging from its size and behavior.

The veterinarians prepared immobilizing drugs, put them in a syringe pole and injected the wolf in the hip from about 10 feet away. A few minutes later, I took out my cable cutter and clipped the snare from its neck. It was a female, and in amazingly good condition considering the stress it was under. The pup's only problem seemed to be a bit of hypothermia.

Next we turned toward the commotion in the brush to our left. Our flashlights revealed a wild-eyed gray wolf, chomping small trees, and spitting out mouthfuls of bark. This one was also a small female – a sub-adult. Between her bouts of thrashing, the vet aimed a needle and injected her, too. Once the drugs took effect, I looked in her mouth and throat to see if I needed to remove wood splinters. She seemed OK.

We moved the wolves to the trucks where the vets struggled to examine their patients in the bad light and tight quarters. I suggested we take them back to Hinton to finish up. Rick tossed the frozen dead ones into the back of his pickup. The bodies hit like blocks of firewood.

The two female wolves spent the next couple of days in large kennels at Switzer Park, where our team fitted them with radio collars. We had to have collars on some of the pack members in order to find them again in the vast wilds of Alberta. We didn't want them spending any more time than necessary in kennels, and it took a while to get the number we needed – seventeen packs in all. The collared wolves would go back to their packs, betraying their locations. It would make things go faster for the capture team to dart several at a time out of each pack.

On December 5, I took the two pups back to the area where they were captured. LuRay Parker went along, hoping to get some good photos on this cold, crisp day. I needed an extra set of hands to help me release the wolves, so Bill Paul, a USDA Wildlife Services* supervisor from Minnesota, was my helper. While LuRay snapped away, Bill and I carried the metal kennels into a meadow and opened them. Neither wolf was eager to leave the calm confines of the box. We waited. Eventually each put a tentative paw on the snow, then bolted out of sight like Wile E. Coyote. The next time they were captured, we figured, they'd be on their way to a new home far away.

*The United States Department of Agriculture Animal Damage Control changed its name to USDA Wildlife Services in 1986. I worked for this agency in Montana from 1975-2001. In the West, its trappers are responsible for killing problem predators. The agency operates under the federal Animal Damage Control Act of 1931. Simply put, it is the hired gun of the livestock industry.

The black pup rescued from Rick's snares, then released, became known as the McLeod River wolf. She was never captured again, even though that was the intent when she was collared. That happened a few times during the two weeks we rounded up wolves for reintroduction – we took the ones we could get. Nevertheless, biologists at Alberta's fish and wildlife division were able to follow the McLeod River wolf's life a bit longer because of the radio collar. They learned a lot about her, including how she died: She spent too much time lurking around a farm and was shot. This incident sprang to mind a lot during the dozens of wolf reintroduction public hearings I attended in Idaho, Wyoming and Montana, where people asked, "Why can't you just leave them in Canada where they're safe?"

When it was time to round up the wolves and get them on planes, the helicopters went up with their telemetry receivers in search of those telltale blips. The louder the sound – like water dripping into a bucket – the closer you are to the wolf. After the biologist had darted a few and retrieved them from the snowy landscape, the wolves needed transporting back to the warehouse at Switzer Park where vet checkups and kennels awaited. It was where all the wolves for reintroduction underwent processing, as we called it. Back and forth, the helicopters went, finding the radio-collared wolves, following them, and getting them out in the open where the animals could be darted and retrieved. It was an all-day affair for a couple of weeks.

On January 9, 1995, the chopper pilot's voice crackled over the radio. His gunner had darted a couple of wolves in the wilderness near Edson, an hour from the park. A trip by air would use too much time and fuel. Someone needs to drive up here and retrieve them, he said. I knew the way. I volunteered.

At the remote airport at Edson, I waited. Soon the hum of a helicopter was in the distance. It buzzed in, sending snow flying in a blinding tornado of white. A couple of guys jumped out and took the wolves out of the back. They bent low with the limp

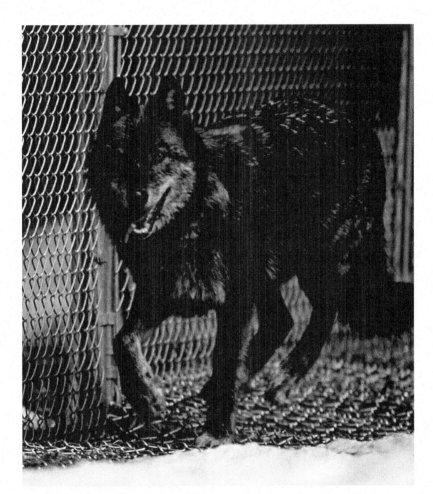

Wolf Number 9 in Yellowstone's Rose Creek pen.
(Photo courtesy Yellowstone National Park)

bodies, one large and black, the other small and gray, hurrying them to my truck.

"Here," I said. I'd cleared the passenger seat of my truck. "Put their heads facing me."

I wanted to keep close to them and monitor their breathing while I drove. Putting them in the back of the truck with below-zero temperatures and blasting wind would freeze them to death. I got in and let their heads rest on my right leg. I put a vial of the sedative, Ketamine, on the dashboard with a syringe and needle next to it, and then pulled out of the parking lot.

The gray wolf had a radio collar, but not the black wolf. I felt the black one's belly. She was an older animal, kind of salt-and-pepper colored, and had been a nursing mother earlier in the year. She was probably the breeding female of her pack, what most folks call the alpha. This was most likely her pup of the year, if they were captured together. I turned up the heater, then rolled my window down a little to keep the wolves from getting too warm, half freezing myself in the process. When they began to stir, I pulled over and gave them a Ketamine booster.

An hour later, I was back in Hinton and a swarm of people came toward me as I parked. An Associated Press photographer asked if she could take a few shots of the wolves before biologists unloaded them. Then the teams weighed, poked and prodded them, making sure they were healthy. On a datasheet they were given identities: R-7F for the young gray one, R-9F for the older black one. The "R" stood for red ear tags, the number stood for the order in which they were run through tests and documented in Switzer Park, and "F" or "M" meant female or male. All of the red ear-tagged wolves went to Yellowstone; "B's" were blue ones, destined for Idaho. We did verbal shorthand almost immediately. The wolves' male or female designation was dropped when we talked about them – R-9F became simply "Number 9" because there was no R-9M.

Biologists, veterinarians and volunteers busied themselves with the wolves I'd just delivered, and others that had been brought in by helicopter. Someone yelled from across our busy warehouse...

"Hey, this Number 7 is the pup you cut out of the snare, Carter."

Well I'll be damned. We might have left the black sister behind, but mom and one pup were together now, and soon would be on a plane to Yellowstone. A robust, 132-pound male wolf, Number 10, was slated to go out on the same flight. The vets thought he just might be a good mate for Number 9.

On a hill behind Yellowstone's historic Buffalo Ranch in Lamar Valley, in the quiet of tall spruce and pines, near a gurgling stream called Rose Creek, park employees and contractors had spent a good amount of sweat and elbow grease building a ten-foot tall fence on an acre of ground. They also installed a few wood kennels that looked like big doghouses. They named it the Rose Creek Pen, and put the first wolves from Canada here to acclimate before their release. It couldn't be seen from the road and was away from the frantic activity of employees readying the most famous national park in the world for its newest residents. After an absence of more than 60 years, the wolves were back. But wolf experts thought that sending them out too soon could lead them to try to find their way north again.

Like other Yellowstone wolves, Number 7, Number 9 and Number 10 were confined at Rose Creek. Biologists fed them road kill, which was hauled there twice a week in a sleigh through many feet of snow by a handlebar-mustached buckaroo named Bob Blackwell and his trusty mules. Like the other wolves, the trio paced the perimeter and seemed uneasy. Everyone was relieved when they started becoming more interested in each other than what was outside the fence. Park employees opened the pen door on March 20, but the wolves had become comfortable and stayed put. On March 29, they left. Radio collars showed that they remained together. And there was one more thing to note: Number 9 was pregnant.

After we'd gotten the wolves on planes in Canada, I went home to my old job in Montana, looking at dead cows and sheep. Yellowstone hired Mike Phillips and Doug Smith as wolf managers, two guys I would see a lot more later.

The three wolves roamed around together for a while in the park, but for whatever reason, decided to head northeast. At some point, Number 7 split off from the group and went her own way, leaving the mated pair to wander close to Red Lodge, Montana. Outside the protection of Yellowstone, wolves live precarious lives, and Number 10 didn't last long. A local redneck, Chad McKittrick, shot the animal, telling federal agents he thought it was a dog or a bear. He cut off the wolf's head and stripped the body of its hide, minus the feet, and threw the rest of the carcass in the brush. He tossed the radio collar into a flooded road culvert. One of McKittrick's pals turned him in and refused the $13,000 federal reward for it. McKittrick was convicted of killing an endangered species and possessing and transporting its body parts. His name is still on the lips of anyone who has followed the history of Yellowstone wolves. As a result of his conviction, the McKittrick Policy emerged, requiring that federal prosecutors prove a defendant knew the biological identity of the animal killed. The policy has since let many wolf poachers slip through the cracks.

By some measure of luck and alignment of stars, Number 9 had wandered like an apparition through farms and ranches, escaping any number of crosshairs. She stayed in the Red Lodge area. She seemed to prefer it. She had no idea that she and the two others were the first wolves to leave the park, or that researchers were worriedly tracking her via radio-collar signals, or that by now she had gained rock-star status. Yellowstone is not fenced, and no one ever promised to keep the wolves from leaving. While most that were released stayed in the park, these three didn't care for it. In fact, Number 9 picked as her home base a nice spread of private ranchland where she was most likely to cause a ruckus. It didn't take long.

A phone call from a rancher in spring 1995 was all it took to mobilize a team to go retrieve Number 9 before she got herself shot. The U.S. Fish and Wildlife Service was not ready for a political debacle this early in reintroduction. The incident with McKittrick and Number 10 had been enough. The office in Helena fielded the rancher's call and soon biologist Joe Fontaine was on his way toward Red Lodge and the area where the female wolf had been reported trotting through foaling pastures. Using his antennae and receiver, Joe followed the wolf's signal, coming to a stand of pines. He heard muffled, tiny whines and then found the den – a depression in the ground covered by low hanging spruce boughs. He counted eight pups, but no mother. She must have slipped away when she heard him approach.

Weeks went by while federal officials wondered what to do next. Moving the mother and pups back to the park seemed like the only logical answer. My phone rang in Helena, and within a day our small capture team had assembled: Doug Smith, Joe Fontaine, veterinarian Dr. Mark Johnson, and me. Videographer George Gentry, and public affairs officer Sharon Rose came along, too. It was only when I was on my way to Red Lodge that I made a couple of inquiries. This was the wolf who rested her head on my leg in Edson, Canada, and whose pup, Number 7, I cut from a snare near the McLeod River.

Doug had been making regular flights south of Red Lodge to keep track of the mother wolf. My assignment was to set foot-hold traps to catch her. On May 15, we went to work, sneaking down an old road where Joe had put out deer carcasses to supplement Number 9's diet. He hoped it would keep her close by and focused on an easy food source. We found her footprints, so I set five traps, or "sets," over a distance of 100 yards. On each trap I tied thin parachute cord that attached to a magnet on a radio collar, which I hung high in a nearby tree, secured with duct tape. When the trap snapped, the cord would pull the magnet off the radio collar, causing it to emit a signal. I baited each set with some stink I brewed up myself. I called it Carter's Kitty Kandy, the main ingredient of which was ground-up bobcat. I also carefully placed a few turds from the Rose Creek Pen. If I were Number 9, I'd find all of this irresistible. We planned to sleep in shifts that night, taking turns monitoring the five radio collars from our rooms at the Super 8 Motel in Red Lodge, several miles away. We would know the moment any one of the traps snapped or moved.

At 4 a.m., Mark Johnson called my room.

"One of the radios went off," he said. I jumped up and got dressed. In 10 minutes, we were all standing in the lobby. The motel manager was as excited as the rest of us. He made a pot of coffee and dug out a box of doughnuts meant for guests who kept more normal breakfast hours.

We waited for first light so we could see what we were doing. Doug telephoned local helicopter pilot Rick Sanford to enlist his help in case we captured the wolf and her pups. When the sky started to look pale, we convoyed to a road about a quarter mile above my trap line. Mark loaded his syringe pole. I hoped I hadn't caught some poor old porcupine or coyote. Everybody always seemed so confident that it would be a wolf. I was optimistic, but I also was a realist. Other animals like the smell of wolf lure – even deer, elk and cattle – and any animal could have approached the baited traps. But my traps were set for the weight of a wolf, which helped minimize the chance of catching anything else.

I walked ahead of Joe and Doug. I wanted the area to stay as undisturbed by people as possible in case we had to go into a second night of trapping. As I walked down the trap line, I could see where one was missing. The cord was draped down the road and into the bushes. I motioned and the others came forward silently.

Doug unpacked his radio receiver and tuned into R-9's frequency. I scanned the dark bushes in front of me and could see that one of the wild roses was bent in an odd direction toward the road. Doug was getting a strong signal, and Joe pointed under a tree that was off to the side, below the road grade. I could see the wolf's black muzzle. She crouched, silent and motionless.

Throughout this adventure, I had my big camcorder going. I'd made it a habit over the years, and there were more than a few times I was damn glad I had video to back up my stories. Somehow, no one else ever seemed to have a camera handy. I zoomed in on the concealed wolf and motioned with one hand. I wanted Joe to move in and inject her. The rose thorns pulled at his coat as he inched down to the wolf twenty feet away. The wolf was unusually calm as he approached her and gave her a sedative. Now that I look back on it, Number 9 was one of the calmest, coolest wolves ever. She never got worked up about anything. Joe and Doug removed the trap from her front foot. She was caught by two toes but had no visible injury. My trap, a McBride #7, did exactly what it was supposed to: catch the wolf low on the foot in the toe webbing. Contrary to what a weekend trapper says, you don't need big bone-crushing traps to catch a wolf. Research trapping had become my specialty, and I expected to be able to release any wolf with nary a limp because I didn't leave them in the trap for long. I was adamant about checking traps at dawn.

I helped lift Number 9 and put her on Doug's shoulders. She was full of milk, which reminded all of us that our job was not finished. Doug walked her back to the trucks where Mark had a tarp spread on the ground, ready to receive his patient.

The Rose Creek pen after a group of wolves were released, 1995.
(Photo courtesy Yellowstone National Park)

We needed to get moving. If we couldn't find the pups, we were going to have to let their mother go. Being only a month old, they were small enough that a few missed feedings could kill them.

Doug and Mark had brought along several long-handled dip nets in the event we had to run down the pups. Spreading out, we moved downslope in the direction of the large spruce tree where Joe had found the pups weeks before. But there were hundreds of spruces to choose from. Joe wasn't sure exactly which one it was. A half-hour into it, we found the shallow depression under the tree, but the pups were gone.

Things looked grim, and the clock was ticking. The country was vast, steep and timbered, and the pups could be anywhere. Then Doug had an idea. While flying and radio tracking Number 9 the afternoon before, he had asked the pilot to line up the airplane with the road where I'd set my traps. When he flew parallel to the road, a radio collar signal blipped on one side. Doug figured that the wolf probably had her pups uphill from the traps, a half mile above the old den site. It was as good an idea as any, so we headed that direction. Joe was frustrated, though. Where in the hell had she moved the pups? We were all getting a little testy. We were tired, hungry, and now it looked like we might blow this capture. We pulled out maps and studied the terrain to the southeast. In the distance, Rick Sanford's chopper landed. Soon he came through the trees, joining the search.

An hour ticked by. At the top of the ridge, we met Joe and the Super 8 manager, who had tagged along because he wanted to be in on things. The manager was breathless. He was sure he'd heard the pups growling and whimpering above us. He and Joe led the way and when we got to the spot, Joe whispered and pointed at an old rockslide.

"Up there."

We picked our way forward, low pine boughs whipping our faces. Joe got down on his belly and reached into the space created between two huge rocks when they slid off the hillside long ago. His arm emerged, and he handed Doug a rabbit-sized wolf pup. Then another and another, and everybody gathered around Joe to help take them. I kept the video camera running. The seven pups huddled in the net, trying to hide their faces.

"You think there's more?" I asked Joe, who had stood up. He couldn't get his arm in there any farther. He shook his head.

"Maybe try one more time," I urged him. Doug's arms were longer so he got down and reached in. Rick handed him a pair of Leatherman pliers.

"I can feel something soft," Doug grunted. He was up to his shoulder. He felt around for several minutes until his pliers pinched shut on something and he pulled it out. One more pup.

The pups were getting cold, and right about the time we were thinking up ways to keep them warm, the motel manager took off his tattered coveralls, knotted the ends of the sleeves and legs and put a couple of pups down each, holding the ends like four handles. He carried the pups to the helicopter like that. A warm, dark place to wait for their mother. In short order, they were all back in the Rose Creek pen.

Later that year, an early August storm ripped through Yellowstone's Lamar Valley with enough force to take down the biggest, oldest trees. Number 9, now known as the matriarch of the Rose Creek pack, panicked and raced around the pen where she once lived with Number 10 and Number 7. Huge spruce trees dropped into their enclosure, bending the metal fence supports into giant horseshoes.

When the storm subsided, Yellowstone's Mike Phillips and Doug Smith high-tailed it to the Rose Creek pen and snuck in to observe the damage. Number 9 paced nervously, and four pups were in one of the wooden boxes, their makeshift den site. But

*Wolf Number 7 awaits release into Yellowstone National Park.
(Photo courtesy National Park Service/Jim Peaco)*

four other pups were missing. Mike and Doug whispered about the trees that had nearly destroyed the pen. One of them lay square across the smashed fence, creating a perfect bridge to the outside world, low enough for four-month old pups to navigate easily. They could be anywhere by now.

My phone rang with news of the escaped pups, and by the next afternoon I was in Yellowstone setting traps. It was a tall order, trapping pups without injuring their feet. Park managers and I agreed that I should use traps known as Soft Catch, with rubber-padded jaws. I would attach makeshift trap monitors like we'd used not too many months before. While we sat in a brief meeting strategizing, I wondered what made these wolves keep appearing in my life. Maybe it was as simple as not enough wolf trappers to go around. I was excited but wary; if I killed puppies in a trap in Yellowstone, the Mecca of wildlife lovers, I was as good as dead, too.

I didn't really know Mike or Doug very well. I thought this trapping opportunity might help our friendship along. We headed out of park headquarters in Mammoth to Lamar Valley's Buffalo Ranch, within a mile of the Rose Creek pen. We hiked in and I set ten traps before dark while Doug and Mike attached radio transmitters to the traps and recorded the frequencies on a makeshift map so we knew which was which. We set up a simple telemetry listening station in the open bed of my pickup, taking advantage of the slight elevation.

Doug parked a government-issued Suburban above the Buffalo Ranch, near the creek crossing. I'd forgotten to bring food, but I figured since this was a Yellowstone deal, they'd have some good chow. Doug and Mike produced old cold cuts and smashed bread from a backpack. We didn't bother with a camp-fire. It was almost too warm for one. Soon a full moon rose over the ridge and we discovered we weren't really ready for sleep. One of them pulled out a deck of cards and, as the night set in, we played game after game of hearts. The moon was so bright that we could read our hands perfectly. Each hour, Doug climbed into the back of my pickup and put on the headphones, hoping to hear a signal.

I didn't wear a watch, but it must have been almost dawn before we decided to get some shut-eye. Mike was the shortest, so he took the front seat, which left Doug and me together in the back under a filthy, sweat-stained horse blanket. The back seat wouldn't fold down flat, so we slept on the lump.

No traps snapped that first night. We climbed a high ridge the next morning to see if we could spy on the wolves and see what was going on. As we ascended single-file, Mike stopped suddenly. Doug and I did a Three Stooges move, nearly running into him. A grizzly bear stood in our path less than forty yards away, motionless. I had never been so close to a free ranging grizzly that didn't have its foot in a snare. If this one decided that we were on the menu, we wouldn't have a prayer. We waited, motionless. The bear resumed its journey, finally ambling over the next ridge.

Evening came again, and again we played hearts under the lantern moon. It was midnight and Doug again plodded to the truck to check for radio signals.

"We've got one!" he yelped.

Backpacks pre-loaded, we started the mile-long hike toward the pen in the dark. Our trek must have looked pretty funny from a distance as we swung our flashlights wildly looking for any grizzly we might surprise.

Just outside the perimeter of the Rose Creek pen, a black wolf pup struggled in one of the traps. Mike and Doug leapt forward and pinned it to the ground. In a second, they had the trap off, then unlocked the pen door and placed the pup inside. We didn't want to create any more ruckus than necessary, so we didn't talk. We made our way back to the Suburban as quietly as we could. Another night under the horse blanket with my new pal, Doug. Mike snickered up front.

The third night two traps snapped. This time we caught a black and a gray pup. One more night might be all we needed to catch the last pup. We thought we'd really accomplished something, and Mike wanted to check all of the traps and count pups in the pen. As we stood outside the damaged enclosure, Number 9 ran around nervously, often dashing within feet of us.

Mike did a headcount and swore. "We're still missing pups!"

He and Doug counted again. There were several missing.

"We're no fucking further ahead than three days ago!"

We all looked at each other. I had to sort of chuckle.

As long as Number 9 remained in the pen, choosing not to use the fallen trees as a way out, the pups were coming and going. Until the trees were sawed up and the fence was repaired, we were wasting our time.

It was just as well that we give it up for now, my new friend Doug said. President Clinton and his family were coming to Yellowstone in a few days to visit the Rose Creek wolves.

"We don't want him seeing a dirty Wildlife Services trapper around our wolves," he said, trying not to grin. "Better pack your shit and get out."

When Number 9's pups weighed 40 or so pounds, they were finally large enough to be radio collared and released with their mother into Yellowstone. Four were male. Four were female. It was this pack that, up until the year 2000, contributed to the bloodlines of nearly 80 percent of the wolves in the park.

On January 16, 2001, I was in Yellowstone on a routine mission, helping Doug helicopter dart descendants of the Rose Creek pack and replace worn-out radio collars. By now, Number 9 was old and frail and her radio collar had quit working, too.

Doug and I talked about what to do if we encountered her during the capture. Neither of us had the heart to bother her anymore. She'd contributed tremendously to wolf recovery in Yellowstone, and Doug decided she deserved to be left alone. Running her hard and putting her through the stress of handling might kill her.

As the chopper zeroed in on the pack's last known location in the vastness of Yellowstone, I saw a wolf standing broadside on a sunny ridge away from the others. She was the distinct silvery-white of an old wolf, the only one like her in the pack. It was Number 9. She looked at me as we passed by, but didn't run. I pulled in my dart gun, and we headed toward the others. They were young, and flew like magic across their bright and snowy home.

Doug and I were among the last to see Number 9. She disappeared some time after that day, and her body was never found. I'd like to think she went peacefully and remained part of Yellowstone.

The Cabin

The Idaho Department of Fish and Game owns an old log cabin and corrals in Bear Valley, nestled in the trees at the edge of the Frank Church-River of No Return Wilderness. I spent a lot of time there in the summers I worked for the state of Idaho after I retired from the U.S. Fish and Wildlife Service. But by then, the cabin and I had known each other a good long while.

I traveled many miles by pickup truck in the 1980s and 1990s working in Montana, Idaho and Wyoming. I was a federal trapper and livestock depredation specialist for Wildlife Services, the predator control arm of the U.S. Department of Agriculture, and over time had become the agency's wolf expert in the Northern Rockies. The job meant I basically lived in my government truck.

People often look at me sideways when I tell them what I did for a living for most of 33 years. They don't realize that being a federal trapper really is a job. When I was supervising a dozen or so of them in Montana, none of them had a college degree. They were simply the guys that the local ranchers already knew. The locals who were private trappers didn't like government trappers much; they saw them as competition. But that didn't matter. The people the feds were hired to please were the ranchers.

Federal trappers came with the territory, literally. People who migrated west behind rickety wagons brought sheep and cattle with them. Somebody had to make the range safe for domesticity, and that's where the federal government stepped in. It was in the economic interests of the country for the West to be settled. Trappers were hired to kill coyotes, wolves, bears, weasels, badgers, beavers and anything else that got in the way of grazing livestock or growing crops. They killed varmints in various ways. Early on, before anybody really thought it out, they used poison baits. But most often, they used steel foot-hold traps, lots of them, followed by a bullet to the head. By the beginning of the 20th century, American settlers and their government had cleared the West of most of the very things that made it interesting, including Native tribes. By the 1930s, most wolves had been poisoned out of existence by the feds – even in places like Yellowstone. It's ironic that some modern Western ranchers, who are often so anti-fed, are the ones who directly benefited from all the ways the feds tamed the place.

I did plenty of coyote and fox killing when I was a trapper. I did it on my own for profit, too. Fur prices were good in the 1960s and '70s, and I took full advantage. It was better than sitting at a desk, and it was what I knew how to do. And really, I loved it. I never hated the animals I trapped and killed; I was just raised in a different environment from the one I encountered during wolf reintroduction. Trapping for profit or out of curiosity was what a guy did. I grew up in rural Iowa and thought trapping a fox was the greatest thing in the world. I have done other things, but not many other things. I am a trapper, and that's how I will always see myself.

Part of being a trapper, as it happens, is that you can't have a lot of needs. Mine are pretty simple, and comfort and convenience were never at the top of the list – mostly because it was pointless. When I was on the road all the time, I was used to

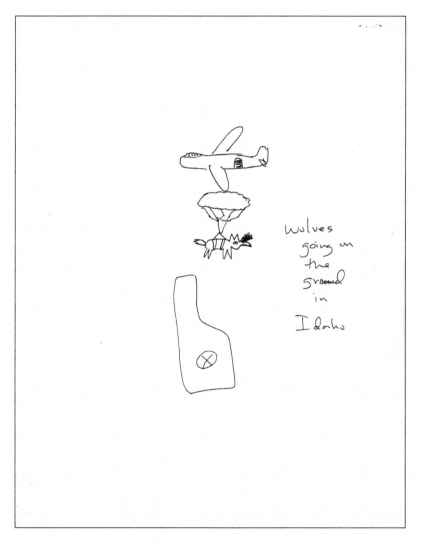

An unknown sketcher's rendering of how reintroduced wolves got to Idaho.
(Collection of Carter Niemeyer)

getting a room at a fleabag motel, or stopping wherever I could find a flat spot for my tent. If I weren't so tall, I might have slept in my truck. In 1993, though, I found myself following reports of wolves in Idaho, and when I hit Bear Valley, my routine changed, however temporarily. From then on, whenever I found myself in the area, I wanted to stay in the old cabin.

The first time I eased my truck into the dirt parking spots in front of the Bear Valley cabin, I met Idaho game warden Rob Brazier, whose feet were sticking out from under the little building like the thing had been dropped on him. Rob was focused on a broken water pipe under the crawl space. The cabin was a victim of many harsh winters, situated as it was in the shade of lodge-pole pines at 6,400 feet elevation. I offered to give him a hand, but there was only room for one person under there. Rob finally emerged with a section of pipe that sported a six inch-long split. He went back under with new pipe he'd scrounged up. That done, he gave me a tour of the place.

The cabin was no larger than 400 square feet, and over the decades, people with differing ideas about how to fix a hole in the floor, or a crack in the ceiling, had all taken a poke at minimal maintenance. A storage shed out back housed an oily propane-powered generator, and my nose told me the place had a serious mouse problem. I almost fell over when Rob opened the shed door and the stink of rodent piss came at us. In one corner were blocks of firewood and a splitting maul. In the other, white gas and funnels for filling lamps and appliances.

A cabin like this one – old and used solely for work assign-ments – isn't what people think. An occasional paint job made the outside look acceptable, but there really was nothing cute about it, mostly because form had followed function for so long. Also, because the government owned the cabin, everything was done as cheaply as possible, right down to the mismatched linoleum squares and butt-sprung mattresses. The generator, the source of life there, was accompanied by a grimy, handwritten note: "Check oil before starting." A truck battery was what made the machine turn over. We flipped switches and primed it, and in short order, the oil-drenched monster chugged to life. As long as it ran, we had two of the greatest inventions of the modern era: water pressure and a hot shower.

Staying in the cabin meant a reprieve from mosquitoes and frequent mountain thunderstorms. Plus, it was nice to sleep on a mattress once in a while – no matter how old and discolored. Another major luxury was having a real toilet. There was a shovel leaning against the wall, however, to remind occupants that septic tank failure was always a possibility. I was never much bothered by all the mice chewing and racing around at night. I just wrapped a pillow around my head if it got too loud.

Rob left, and I was alone. I was there to meet with a group from the Wolf Recovery Foundation, the first organization completely dedicated to the restoration of wolves in the Northern Rockies. Volunteers, headed by director Suzanne Laverty (later Suzanne Stone) were here because they wanted desperately to confirm several sightings of wild wolves in and around the wilderness, and Bear Valley in particular. I'd gotten the green light to help out from the U.S. Fish and Wildlife Service in Helena, where I was based, and where the federal Northern Rockies wolf program was headquartered. I knew how to find wolves; I'd learned out of necessity. Because of that, Suzanne wanted me to come to Idaho to see if wolves were there. So I climbed in my truck and made the journey.

I checked phone messages on the way, stopping at phone booths here and there, hoping I could keep too many messages from piling up. A Montana game warden wanted me to check out a couple of dead sheep near Philipsburg, Montana, so I veered off my route long enough to examine them – two dead lambs each weighing about 60 pounds. I wasn't sure whether a wolf killed the lambs or if large dogs were involved. With the rancher's permission, I took the carcasses with me to Idaho where I could spend more time looking them over. In the meantime, maybe he would find more evidence of dogs or wolves around his ranch. We grabbed the lambs by the legs and slung them into my pickup bed.

I made it to the Bear Valley cabin the next day, shortly before the herd of wolf foundation volunteers. We exchanged handshakes and pleasantries out among the parked cars, but it wasn't long before one of them, Roy Ferrar, wandered over and discovered the dead lambs in the back of my pickup. I saw him out of the corner of my eye. He called to his wife, pointing at the scene he'd discovered. He seemed fascinated and troubled, wondering out loud what my plans were. Soon others were leaning over the pickup bed looking at the bloated, bloody animals. What better way to explain what kind of work I did. I joined them and pointed out the wounds, explaining that wolves in Montana were supposedly the prime suspects.

Being a federal trapper among greenies, my motives were suspect. Wolf advocates figured my sole goal in life was to kill things, and this group wasn't shy about ripping into me about it. And who drives around with dead animals in his pickup? I have to admit that I had spent an awful lot of time both killing animals and driving around with dead ones because it was part of my job. But over time, I surprised even myself. I discovered that I'd changed my attitude. While my supervisors wanted a body count, I wanted answers. We were constantly at odds. I fought back, especially when it came to wolves. A wolf didn't deserve to die just because it was a wolf. I wanted to know what exactly was responsible for the dead livestock I examined. I expected everybody to feel this way, even if it meant that wolves were guilty – because sometimes they were, and sometimes I had to kill wolves because of it. But most of the time, dead livestock was not the fault of predators. So when I arrived at Bear Valley to meet with these people, I pretty much knew what they were thinking.

"OK, so what's this?" demanded volunteer Gin MacDonald. We'd left behind the charms of my pickup truck when it began to rain. She appeared beside me in the cabin's kitchen, tossing a chunk of canine shit in the sink.

"Coyote." I said. No hesitation.

"Not wolf?" she countered.

"Nope," I said. "That's coyote shit."

Her eyes narrowed as she gathered up the specimen. I guessed she knew what it was. She wanted to see if I knew, too. She seemed pissed off that I was so sure.

Hoo boy, this could be a long weekend, I thought.

That evening the rain turned into a downpour, but we stuck to our plans and traveled muddy roads at dusk, searching for areas where wolves might cut through. I howled into a dark valley that rolled away into wilderness. There was no answer, but I aggravated a colony of beavers and they slapped their tails in response. The chance of a chattering group seeing or hearing wolves is slight. The chance of a group finding wolves by picking a random spot to howl, not having anything else to go on, is even more remote. Wolves can cover a hell of a lot of ground in one night. If you want to encounter them, you have to be where they're headed, not where they've been, and that's hard to know unless you find wolf sign: howling from a certain area, or fresh tracks or shit. Still, this was a chance for me to get to know people who were solely interested in bringing back the wolf. I admired their dedication, even though I didn't understand their lifestyles or attitudes, or necessarily agree with their politics. I never knew people like this until I started working in the wolf arena in Montana. I never thought I'd have any reason to rub shoulders with folks like that, and I could tell they were suspicious of me, especially the women.

Conversation lagged, but the rain didn't. We ended up stuffed in the cabin together, about eight of us in a place designed for four, comfortably. We lit the woodstove and made small talk about camping and building fires. I decided we needed a better topic, so I suggested that Ross Perot would make a great president, with Rush Limbaugh as his running mate. Everyone stared at me. Then the room exploded in disgust and I leaned back in my chair and chuckled. Before I knew it, my little portable clock said it was past midnight. We'd spent hours talking, not about politics, but about wolf biology and the likelihood that wandering wolves could survive the crosshairs in Idaho long enough to breed – to become a naturally occurring, viable population. I had to admit that I thought it sounded like a long shot. If there were more places like Bear Valley, large predators would have half the battle won. But even a big, wild, relatively isolated place was no guarantee that the life of any wolf would be a long one.

"It's going to be whatever the hook-and-bullet bunch want. That's where the money to manage wolves will come from," I said. There were a lot of long faces in the dim light.

Before the last lantern was turned down, we'd covered a lot of ground. The group moved from worrying about what I did for a living to worrying about what they could do as citizens to truly help wolves. They seemed hungry for a peek into what's real for wolves outside of Yellowstone. And whether we meant to or not, we had become friends. There was barely room to turn around in the cabin, and a few people decided it would be easier to sleep in their cars. But morning came quickly, and with it breakfast and more talk. The rain had made huge, muddy puddles everywhere, but the cabin only leaked a little. When somebody needed to do dishes or take a shower, I fired up the generator the way Rob had showed me.

We never did find any wolves in Bear Valley that weekend. Our timing and the weather kept us from them. I wondered later if they really expected me to produce a wolf on demand. Maybe this had been about something else. Maybe it was about bridging a gap.

At the time, I considered myself on the ranchers' side, even though I enjoyed seeing and hearing wolves, rare as they were. But unlike a lot of the guys I knew and worked with, I liked meeting new people, even, and maybe especially, if I didn't agree with their ideas. It was fun to bat around ideas. Maybe that's what this group needed, too. My new friends had a lot of work ahead if they wanted wolves back, but maybe what they needed more than finding a wolf to howl at was a friend from the other side. They wanted wolves to be given a chance at a comeback. I wasn't too sure how it would go, but I thought about it plenty. I wanted wolves to have a chance, too.

Early morning trap check in the mountains.
(Photo by Carter Niemeyer)

Number 27

A radio collar that hangs on my wall at home has an aluminum dart stuck in it that no amount of pulling will remove. It was a dart meant for immobilizing a wolf. I shot that dart in Yellowstone National Park one day in 1997, but by the time the day was through, the wolf, known as Number 27, was dead. Dr. Doug Smith, who now heads Yellowstone's wolf program, gave me the collar after it was all over. He didn't say much. He knew it didn't end the way I wanted. He was right in thinking that the collar served as a souvenir of admiration rather than dominance over that wolf. It's a plaintive reminder of a tough animal that we failed to change.

In January 1996, a helicopter capture team searching for wolves near Pink Mountain, British Columbia, spotted Number 27 and her pack – the Halfway pack – feeding on a bison carcass in the Halfway River watershed. The team saw seven wolves, all gray. At the time, she and the others were known only to each other and to the wild. There were no names. But by the end of the week, all of them had been darted, collared and placed in captivity, soon to be transported to Yellowstone and central Idaho. There they would be set free in a great experiment by the United States government to right an old wrong: returning an apex predator to America's mountain west.

Number 27 was the dominant female of the group, the "alpha," a silver-white wolf in charge of the others. This is often the case with the breeding female, and in fact the pack may split up if she goes missing. The rest included her mate and their pups and one young wolf from a previous litter. The capture team had a story about this wolf: Twice during the pursuit she turned and leaped at the helicopter, mouth open, snarling. But like all wolves that go up against helicopters, she lost. Once collared and measured, she became known on the datasheets as Number 27. She and her mate, Number 28, were two of the largest captured, weighing 115 and 130 pounds, respectively.

In Yellowstone, Number 27 and her pack (minus a young female that was destined for Idaho) were kept in a fenced enclosure along Nez Perce Creek in Yellowstone's Firehole River Valley and were renamed the Nez Perce pack. For ten weeks, they saw few humans and were fed elk and bison meat. Scientists hoped that the wolves' time in holding pens here – as on the other side of the park at Rose Creek – would bond them to their new home, erasing any natural inclination to navigate their way back to Canada.

But on April 2, 1996, the Nez Perce pack got off to a bad start. Biologists opened the Nez Perce pen gate and the female wolves left, led by Number 27. The males hesitated for another two days. As a result, they were lost from each other. Number 27 headed northeast, leading her daughters at a quick clip of 33 miles per day, straight out of the park. They ended up near Red Lodge, Montana. Number 27 was pregnant, and by April 10, the tracking collars showed that she split off from her daughters and wandered widely. She seemed to be spending a lot of time near the small town of Nye. Yellowstone officials worried about her; they wanted her rounded up and returned to the Nez Perce pen. In mid-May they called me for help.

Nye is the Wild West, nestled at the foot of the Beartooth Mountains and not much more than a stone's throw from the Crow Indian Reservation. Residents can't look out the window without seeing rugged landscape. There are ranches, a few little businesses, a mine, and a one-room schoolhouse. Nye's 200 or so people are the kind who are capable of getting through, and possibly enjoying, the area's bitterly cold winters. When a wolf showed up here, it was big news, and people dropped everything to attend community hall meetings about the hell they expected to break loose. It was only a matter of time before Number 27 would kill livestock, they said. Thirty or forty residents – all that would fit in the room – roasted Mike Phillips, the Yellowstone project leader, until he stepped offstage and went outside for some air. I stood at the edge of the room in case I needed to answer questions, then followed Mike out the door. Ed Bangs, the project leader for all Northern Rockies wolves outside the park, got up and took over as the punching bag. Outside, Mike paced around and cut loose with a few expletives about the audience.

"It's a little different outside the park, ain't it?" I smiled. People put on a show if you give them a stage. Many complained that officials promised that no wolves would leave Yellowstone, but that was never the case. Others suggested we all find real jobs. They might have been nice folks normally, but when it came to this topic they were rude and nasty. Not the kind of farm folks I was used to when I was growing up in Iowa.

While the meetings were fine and gave people a chance to berate the feds, it didn't change the fact that if Phillips wanted

Number 27 back in the park we needed to find her den soon. I drove and hiked all over the place with Phillips, Bangs and Smith, scouring the countryside near Nye where the now-infamous silver wolf was last seen. Pilot Roger Stradley had located her collar signal frequently on his almost daily monitoring flights for the park's wolf program. From the air, a wolf's collar emitted a signal for 20 miles or more – if nothing was in the way. From the ground, it was a different story. Telemetry operates on line-of-sight, and often is useless if you are standing on the ground at the base of mountains. Roger had the best vantage point, flying his little plane high over steep, snowcapped peaks, broken forests and open meadows. He could pinpoint an animal's location with astounding accuracy. There were no GPS units then, and Roger would radio back with the wolf's location based on the detailed topographical maps he was never without.

That specificity didn't stop our difficulties on the ground. We searched for Number 27. Then searched some more. Then it started to rain, making it impossible to find tracks. We found nothing. We were starting to wonder if she really had pups at all, but in mid-June, rancher Vern Keller called. Something had killed a sheep in his pasture near Fishtail, just west of Nye.

I'd known Vern and his wife, Averill, for a while. Despite the fact that we met because of wolf trouble, they were always courteous, and we enjoyed talking about ranching and all the troubles that go with trying to raise animals in proximity to grizzly – and now wolf – country. Averill usually hounded me about how bad the wolves were, and then sent me away with a paper plate heaped with homemade cookies. We agreed to disagree. It wasn't personal.

On this day, I rendezvoused with the local federal trapper who had gone on the initial call about the dead sheep. We knocked on the Kellers' door. We needed to get this handled. It was already all over the newspapers and evening news, and Vern Keller's high profile as a state legislator didn't help the wolf's cause. We examined the dead sheep and I decided that the bites

Wolf Number 27 immediately after being darted near Dean, Montana.
(Photo by Carter Niemeyer)

on its neck and hindquarters looked like the work of a wolf. For nearly ten years it had been my job to make decisions like that, and let the supervisors decide whether predators should live or die. Now that we had reintroduced wolves, my phone rang all the time and I was on the road nearly every day, driving all over the place looking at dead cows, sheep, horses, llamas – even rabbits. Everything that tipped over was blamed on wolves, it seemed. We got rid of those varmints for a reason, many ranchers said.

Doug Smith gave me the latest telemetry locations and it looked like Number 27 had been hanging around the Keller ranch, but so had another wolf, Number 15, one of the first wolves captured in Canada during reintroduction, a male I'd dubbed Carter's Hope in a sentimental moment. Wolves liked to leave the park, it seemed, and they were headed north, more or less. Maybe their drive to return home was stronger than everyone thought.

I set traps on July 6 near the Kellers' sheep pasture and along a jeep trail several miles to the west. Instead of my target, Number 27, I caught Number 15. I sent him with Phillips and Smith back to Yellowstone. It was one less wolf around the ranch, anyway. But now Number 27 was on the move again. She was like a phantom. First, here, then there, in Nye, then Fishtail, never staying in one place more than a day or two. We only knew her whereabouts because of all the fixed-wing flying that Roger did. He kept us on track, which kept the pressure on me to catch her.

A half dozen of us, including volunteers from the Yellowstone Wolf Project, walked for miles in steep, timbered country looking and listening for wolf pups. Number 27's constant movement made all of us wonder if she really had any. I checked every location Roger gave me, and set several trap lines, but where she once was, she didn't return. I let my traps sit. Maybe she would make a circle in a week or so. Early on the morning of July 9, a helicopter at the Montana Department of Livestock was suddenly available. It normally was used to gun down coyotes.

I checked on whether we had a recent location on Number 27. I didn't have much time to decide. The chopper was available right now. If I went, it would mean leaving my trap line unchecked that morning, something I wasn't comfortable doing. But the wolf's location appeared to be far from my traps, and if she had pups, they would be far away, too. I got ready, mixed immobilizing drugs and met pilot Tim Graff. I'd check my traps when I returned later that afternoon.

As we circled thick aspen stands and dense brush, I finally got my first good look at Number 27. It was going to be a tough shot. Tim dropped down and I was leveling the dart gun at her when she whirled around on her hind legs and began leaping at the helicopter. She snarled and snapped at us. I'd never seen behavior like this in a wolf. I couldn't dart her because I might hit her in the face. She quit attacking and ran into a patch of forest that was coming up fast. We lost sight of her and gave up the chase.

When we landed, the local federal trapper said horseback riders that morning reported seeing what looked like a wolf pup in a trap. My heart skipped.

"Goddammit!" I yelled at myself. I'd made a stupid decision. I let this happen. It was proof that the pups did, in fact, exist.

It took an hour to get to my traps and check them. I took two Yellowstone volunteers with me. Near the road sat a wolf pup that looked to be about 12 weeks old, about 20 pounds. It was caught by a front foot. I never mean to catch a pup. The tension on traps was adjustable and I always kept them set to keep from catching small non-target animals and birds. The pup's foot was swollen. I grasped it by the scruff of its neck and compressed the trap springs, freeing it, but still hanging on. The foot looked terrible.

"You guys get this fella to the park quick," I handed the pup to the volunteers. "Call Doug and tell him you need a vet."

I agonized over the pup all day. That trap injury should never have happened. I should have checked my traps instead of flying. I never let my traps go unchecked each morning. Never. How could I be so foolish? I had talked myself into thinking there were no wolf pups there. What was one that small doing on the trail? Why didn't the pan tension spring prevent the pup from triggering the trap? I muttered and stewed about all of these things. Soon U.S. Fish and Wildlife Service law enforcement agents called. They wanted to interview me about the incident, just to cover their butts. This was high-profile stuff. I pulled my traps from the area. It was just as well. Roger, on his latest flight, spotted Number 27 far away, cutting across a high mountain meadow, three pups scrambling behind her. The incident with the trapped puppy must have sent her packing.

But the bad news just kept coming.

The trapped pup would have to lose its leg at the shoulder or be euthanized, according to the vet. Doug Smith and Mike Phillips wanted my opinion. Kill it? Because of my screw-up? Hell no. The Wildlife Services state director disagreed. He didn't want the agency getting a black eye over this.

No, I said.

I guess I talked the decision-makers into it. The pup's leg was amputated, and he was sent to a wolf sanctuary in Minnesota to live out his life. A couple of weeks later, my boss tossed a poster on my desk showing a three-legged wolf pup nicknamed "Tripod." They were appearing all over the place. An animal rights group in Bozeman, the Predator Project, had used the incident to illustrate just exactly how inept I was. How inept we all were. True to his nature, Ed Bangs took the blame in the newspapers and tried to explain it away. But I was responsible. I couldn't forgive such a stupid mistake. Years later, I was told the pup lived a long life with other captive wolves.

Meanwhile, we were still empty-handed. Number 27, the mother wolf that had raised pups by herself outside the protection of Yellowstone, had essentially vanished. We could find her radio signal, but she was in high, wild country, wandering the wilderness, leaving no clues that might lead us to her pups. But I kept looking. On August 4, as I continued following wolf tracks, I found what I believed to be wolf pup shit in a boggy area. I hung a radio collar in a nearby tree as a sort of early GPS locator and left. I asked Roger about flying the next morning to see if Number 27 was anywhere close to my radio collar. She was. I returned quietly and set 11 rubber-padded traps. Still, I only came up with one of her pups. This one suffered no injury and we sent it back to Yellowstone. Biologists put it in the pen temporarily, but then released it. The following month, a car hit the pup and killed it.

Number 27 seemed to know we were after her and moved her remaining pups to higher ground. My heart was not in this anymore. She was winning despite all the odds. I respected her for it. At the same time, it pissed me off. I hiked close to her latest known location and set traps only to have her move even higher into dense, roadless forest. No roads meant I couldn't find her tracks in the dust. Also, she seemed to be trap-wise. I needed to call it quits and attend to other, more serious problems between wolves and livestock along the Rocky Mountain front, but by now the Number 27 thing was a contest to see who would win, and my supervisor at Wildlife Services was leading the charge. Things got hotter in the following weeks after Number 27 was seen dragging a lamb under the Kellers' fence, and then was accused of killing a dozen sheep. Defenders of Wildlife, a nonprofit that had been influential in making reintroduction happen, used its compensation fund to pay the Kellers full market value for their sheep. I used that as a reason to put the whole thing on the back burner for a while. Officials at the park agreed to let things simmer down.

Winter set in and the Kellers moved their sheep closer to home. Early in January 1997, my phone rang.

"I was flying today and found that old Number 27, near Roscoe." Roger Stradley sounded pretty excited. "She's right out in the open, Carter. I think you could get her. There's no cover for miles."

But a winter storm had blown in and no helicopter was going up. Ten days later, Roger called again. Now she was northwest of Dean, Montana. She was staying north and west of the park, but not by much.

I had just received a new shipment of the immobilizing drug Telazol and drove to a veterinary clinic in Helena to pick up propylene glycol. I learned about using this non-toxic antifreeze when we were darting wolves in Canada at temperatures well below zero. It is used as a solvent in many pharmaceuticals. Without some kind of antifreeze, the contents of the metal darts would solidify and the darts would not function. The knowledge came in handy when I was about to try again for Number 27.

The snowstorm subsided on January 16, and I made a phone call to get things rolling. I arrived at the Columbus, Montana airstrip just before dawn. The chopper was there. So was Doug Smith from Yellowstone, and we got busy mixing up the darts. A half dozen others were there to help or write about it for various publications. Then Roger radioed in. Number 27 was on a snowy ridge northwest of Dean, 20 miles away. Bob Hawkins lifted the chopper into the air, sweeping us away in a white swirl and into the early blue light.

In the distance, I saw Roger's yellow plane circling. He was above the wolf. We landed briefly and removed my door so I would have a clear shooting platform. Once we were up again, it was only minutes before I had Number 27 in my sights. But when we zoomed in on her, she whirled and tried to attack the helicopter. What was it with this wolf and helicopters? We slowed to stay behind her. Then she turned and ran for her life. Bob sped us toward her and got me down close. I fired. The dart landed in her left hip. She angled away from us, then stopped, then curled into a ball in the snow and didn't move. Bob maneuvered the chopper behind her so we could snap a photo with his ship in the background before he helped me lift her into the backseat. On our return, I could see that more people had assembled where we planned to land along a county road. At the landing spot, Doug and others unloaded Number 27 and moved the wolf to a truck for the ride back to Yellowstone.

Two weeks after Number 27's capture, her former mate, Number 28, was found dead in the Madison River, well outside of Yellowstone's western boundary. His radio collar showed that he had become a lone wanderer after his release in April, but more recently the collar showed that he hadn't moved. Searchers followed the signal to his frozen body. He had been illegally shot and dumped in the river. That made me feel a little better about bringing in Number 27, despite the ridiculous amount of money the feds had spent on the chase. A month later, I darted one more of her pups at the Keller ranch. We couldn't find the other pups, but the Kellers reported no more dead livestock.

It was a rare day. I was home in Helena, getting ready for hunting season. I looked forward to having a bit of time off. But then my phone rang with the news that Number 27 might be in trouble again.

"In fact," said Doug Smith, "we've got a bunch of wolves on walkabout over by West Yellowstone. Ten of them. I'm not sure where they're going, but we're probably going to have to deal with this if they don't come back on their own."

We talked about which wolves, and Doug described a strange conglomeration that had recently been released from the Nez Perce pen. The leader of the group was, of course, Number 27.

Most wolves are shy, but Number 27 acted the way most people think wolves act: confrontational. "She was the only wolf that stood me down in a pen, curled her lip and wouldn't get out of the way when I approached," Doug said. "I walked around her."

On this sortie, Doug believed the others were just following the ringleader. All 10 wolves had been confined in the one-acre Nez Perce pen since Number 27 was darted in January. The other wolves were Number 27's daughter from Canada, Number 37, and three of 37's un-collared pups, which she had raised in the pen. Also with them was Number 29, which was not only 37's brother but – strange for wolves – also the father of her pups. Other escapees from the pen were three yearlings from the Sawtooth pack I'd darted near Augusta, Montana, because their parents had killed livestock. They were Numbers 67, a female, and 70 and 72, both males. The tenth wolf was Number 71, another Sawtooth yearling female that died near Ruby Reservoir, east of Dillon, shortly after the walkabout began. She triggered an M-44 set by a Wildlife Services trapper. The lipstick-sized device is placed on the ground and scented with lure to attract and destroy coyotes in sheep country. When the animal bites down on it, the device shoots sodium cyanide powder into the coyote's mouth, killing it almost instantly.

I really didn't think the park needed my help again, at least I hoped not. Anyway, I had other work to do. I had visions of Number 27 leading her gang, outlaw style, through the mountains, never to be seen again, or eventually deciding Yellowstone was a good enough place to live and circling back to it.

But by the time I returned to Helena, nothing had changed other than the wolves' location. Roger Stradley had been shadowing them in his plane, and at a meeting in Helena, he pointed at his maps. Since September, they'd gone from Hayden Valley in Yellowstone through the Wall Creek Game Range, south to Ennis, over to the Centennial Valley and finally were hanging around the Sage Creek area south of Dillon, Montana. The renegades had killed at least two calves, according to the area's federal trapper.

Ed Bangs, fed up with the drama, drew the line.

"Bring them all in, but I want you to shoot Number 27," he said. "Enough already."

In a chase, animals are no match for helicopters. Only weather can stop those machines. Still, pilot Tim Graff and I packed our gear in the Hughes 500 and took off from Helena into heavy snow and poor visibility. I thought we might have to call it off, a stay of execution for Number 27, until Graff expertly maneuvered us over the blinking power-line beacons at the rocky and unforgiving Boulder Pass. He took it slow, sometimes hovering at a standstill in the whiteness around us, then inching the chopper forward a few feet at a time. We could see the beacons blinking, but barely. Tim was a National Guard flight instructor, so I had faith in him, but I still said my prayers. I wondered about all of us. Why do we put our lives at risk over wolves?

When Interstate 15 came into view, we followed it south, still in a near-whiteout. Within an hour, as we approached Dillon, the storm ceiling began to lift, revealing brilliant blue. But then an even more vicious storm hit. We had to land and wait until the next morning to get going in earnest. The weather was still nasty the next day, but by late morning, Roger Stradley, our spotter, said he wanted to chance it. He picked his way through the rugged mountains below the cloud line in his yellow plane. We ate lunch and waited for his report.

By now, word about the capture attempt had gotten out and a few more biologists and wolf fans showed up to see what was happening. When Roger touched down, he said the visibility was terrible, but he'd found the wolves.

"I had my wings in the clouds and my wheels in the sage-brush when I went over them," he said, nearly out of breath. The man was practically a stunt pilot.

We waited for the storm to subside, and finally went up at three o'clock. I put the darts inside my coat pocket to keep them warm. I put the shotgun in its slot. We'd removed the helicopter door and I stayed just shy of freezing. The ground crew drove down the Interstate and found a field where we could land on our return, then waited there with kennels to take the escapees back to Yellowstone once again.

We had a lot of wolves to dart and I was tense because we were flying in less than ideal terrain. Rolling, steep hills, scattered trees, sagebrush. I took a deep breath and focused out the door.

The action came fast. Wolves ran up little draws and ducked under bushes. We focused on a black wolf first. I aimed and hit it. Roger flew above us and kept track of the drugged wolves so we could go back and find them shortly. Next we cruised up on a small gray pup not wearing a radio collar. I hit it, too. The next wolf in my sights was up ahead. It was Number 27.

I was supposed to kill her, so I should have been reaching for my shotgun, but I thought I'd rather dart her and let the ground crew do the killing. I was tired of it. I had a lot of respect for this old girl. She'd earned it simply by staying alive outside of Yellowstone. Tim brought me alongside her and I fired. The dart went into her collar. At 15 yards, I'd missed what I was aiming for: her shoulder. I couldn't believe my eyes. I reloaded fast, but she ducked into thick timber and disappeared.

We U turned and found three more wolves, which I hit with three more darts. We landed and picked up all of them, thanks to the pilots' sharp eyes. In a couple of trips, we delivered the wolves to the waiting ground crew. Later in the day, we captured one more of the renegades as we headed toward Dillon.

I'd darted six wolves, but Number 27 was still in the timber. Graff and I finally had to land and walk around, hoping to flush her from the trees.

Then, suddenly she was running again, Stradley's voice crackled over the radio. We jumped in the chopper and took off. I put down the dart gun and pulled the shotgun from its holder. I pointed it out the door.

The nearly white Number 27 ran like she was young. She might have kept on into another patch of timber except that she came to an old fence. She must not have seen it because at full speed she bounced off it backward. She regained her footing like a jackrabbit and ran alongside the wire.

We were on her. She didn't have a chance. Not anymore.

I fired twice. I wanted it to be quick.

We landed. Tim wanted a photo, but I said no full-body pictures. I didn't want this moment glorified. I knelt beside her and took a photo of the dart in her collar. I looked at her teeth. They were worn and broken from her time in the metal cages in Canada and from going up against her pen's chain link fence in Yellowstone. That happened to a lot of the wolves we moved. They are wild and don't take to being caged, even if it means breaking off their teeth in an attempt to escape. We put her limp, bloody body in a black garbage bag. What an end for such a survivor.

Not long after the death of Number 27, Number 29, who had been a faithful follower, climbed out of the Nez Perce pen. He was free, but he waited, pacing, until his mate, Number 37, climbed the fence, too. They ran off together. They had learned from the best.

Wolf Number 27 and Bob Hawkin's helicopter, Dean Montana.
(Photo by Carter Niemeyer)

Chaos at 3 a.m.

In August 1997, north of Pinedale, Wyoming, a rancher thought a wolf was killing his sheep on a federal grazing allotment in the Gros Ventre wilderness. But the federal Wildlife Services bosses in Wyoming weren't exactly sure a wolf was guilty. Grizzlies had been troublemakers in the area, too. It was my job to find out, so I got in my truck in Helena, Montana, and started driving, wondering how many more years it would be before folks wised up. Wilderness is not for domestic livestock.

By the time I reached the Idaho border, I'd run out of daylight. In the border town of Tetonia, I stopped to make some calls. The sign said 250 people lived here, but it was pretty quiet. The phone booth had a million-dollar view. Final slivers of pink daylight glowed on the Teton Mountains, the backdrop for the eastern edge of town.

I stepped out of my truck and stretched. A guy was using the phone. I glanced at his truck plates. Federal. A shovel was sticking out of the back and a mess of metal boxes and other gear littered the truck bed. I strolled by the truck's rolled-down window. A couple of guns lay on the seat. This had to be the local federal trapper.

The man turned around and his face lit up. He hung up the phone and pushed his greasy hat back.

"Hey, Carter, what are you doing over here?" We gripped hands. Lee Czapenski was the trapper out of Rexburg, only 30 or so miles away.

"Hey, you wanna see something?" He motioned for me to follow him and pointed at the passenger door of his truck.

A bear track was pressed into the dust. A grizzly, I guessed.

"Look at my damn truck!" Lee said. My eyes followed his hand. Part of the door frame was bent and the outside mirror was shattered. There was more. Lee opened the door and showed me the chewed up headrest, full of punctures. Foam rubber bulged from the seat's injuries.

"I'll tell you one thing, don't shoot a griz in the ass with a rubber bullet." He sort of laughed. He'd been on the phone reporting the damage, which had happened a few hours earlier. He and an Idaho Department of Fish and Game biologist had used a culvert trap to capture and relocate the bear. When they opened the trap on a remote road, they thought shooting the grizzly with a rubber bullet would make it take off faster. Instead, it made a U-turn and attacked Lee's truck. The two men, who'd had the foresight to stay in the truck's cab, dove to the floorboard as the bear tried to climb through the passenger window and take a swipe at them. Lee found his handgun and fired a shot through the open driver's side window, scaring the bear away.

I hoped my trip to Wyoming wouldn't be that exciting.

I stayed in Tetonia that night because I wasn't sure where I might find another gas station. I was on the road early the next morning, and in a few hours was standing over dead sheep on the grazing allotment in the Gros Ventre Wilderness. The Gros Ventre is one of the wildest, most rugged places in the lower

48 states. Predators of all sizes live here, but so do a bunch of domestic sheep, if only for the summer grazing season. I met Merrill Nelson, the Wyoming Wildlife Services district supervisor, and we went over what had happened. We found a place to make camp and he rolled out his sleeping bag on the ground and tied up his two horses alongside the herder's wagon. We straddled an invisible line that divided ordinary Forest Service land, where almost any activity is allowed, and federal wilderness, where you can't take machinery, generally. The seven-mile long road we traveled, barely wide enough for a truck, dead-ended here.

Ranchers who have purchased grazing allotments on federal lands can turn their stock loose in late spring to graze for a fraction of what it costs in other parts of the country. Some of the grazing allotments are generations old. The federal government doesn't really charge enough to pay for the program, but somehow it survives. Western public grazing practices are propped up by the Animal Damage Control Act of 1931, because when you put cows and sheep in wild areas that contain grizzly bears, mountain lions, wolves, and a variety of poisonous weeds that are really just wildflowers, the livestock is going to need help staying alive. That's where the federal trappers come in, and that's why Merrill and I found ourselves in the middle of nowhere with a bunch of stinking, dead sheep.

"Wolf-dog." Robert, the Navajo herder, spoke little English, but tried to tell what he'd seen. He gestured that he'd chased it off, but it returned from the north and killed sheep. He made bigger gestures, describing the grizzly bear that also had taken a toll on the sheep band.

Merrill and I walked the woods. Some of the dozens of dead sheep were obvious bear-kills: bite wounds on their backs and shoulders. Others had been lightly bitten around the neck and hindquarters the way a wolf would kill. The vegetation around the carcasses was packed down the way only a really big animal could accomplish.

"This wolf has to be a wimp," I said. I examined the superficial bites. A wolf was capable of a lot more. But I couldn't find a track. The ground was either rocky or covered with long grass, obscuring whatever had walked there. Maybe I'll just set a few traps and see what I catch, I told Merrill.

We made our way back to camp to find that the horses had run off. I didn't mess with horses. Pretty to look at, but when something like this happened, I was glad I didn't have them to worry about. We agreed to split up. I unloaded my ATV and heaped a few traps on the back. Merrill, grumbling, wandered after the horses. The herder, unsure, followed.

I didn't have much to go on. The wolf was coming from the north – wilderness – straight into the sheep bed grounds, according to the herder. I decided to start there. I dug six traps into everything that looked like a natural corridor, mainly the valleys between ridges. As I returned to camp, Merrill and the herder appeared with the horses.

Merrill offered to make supper, an offer I've never been known to refuse. It sure beat a can of Beanie Weenies. I put up my teepee in the tree line above camp as the sun was setting. It's the best way to hear wolves: get up high and away from gurgling streams. We sat and ate in this place, far away from civilization, with craggy, little known peaks only a short hike to the west. I wrote in my field diary about the "Pinedale" wolf. Wolves outside of Yellowstone are usually named after the closest geographic feature. I didn't know the names of the beautiful, silent mountains that surrounded me tonight. Pinedale seemed good enough.

In the blackness of night, I heard a sound. I hoped I wasn't dreaming. I sat up. A wolf howled. Three times. Then silence. After a few minutes, I lay down again. I was awake now, thinking that at least I know I really am after a wolf. I drifted off, and it seemed like an hour later when I heard sheep bleating and running. Then the guard dog started barking. The chaos went on for a half hour. Then silence. I looked at the small portable clock I always carried in my duffel bag. It was 3 a.m.

At 6 a.m., it was finally light enough to see. I was getting dressed when Merrill talked through my tent.

"Something got into the sheep last night. We've got more dead ones."

"It was a wolf," I said, stepping outside.

He looked at me like I was being funny.

"Now how do you know that?"

"It howled. Didn't you hear it?"

"Are you sure it wasn't my hound? He does that sometimes at night," Merrill said. "I can't believe a wolf howled and I didn't hear it."

But it happens a lot. Heavy sleepers snore right through that haunting sound. I also told him about the sheep stampede and the guard dog barking, which he didn't hear either.

"Well, I'll go with you and check traps and then we can have ourselves a big breakfast," Merrill grinned, emphasizing "big." I started the ATV and he climbed on the back. I loaded my capture gear wherever it would fit. I could tell that my partner thought he was humoring me.

We motored along from one trap to the next, one valley to the next. Nothing. I started thinking maybe Merrill was right and breakfast really was going to be the highlight of the day.

We went up and then down the last ridge. I wasn't too sure where I'd set the last trap. I hadn't marked it with a ribbon nearby like I usually do. I was slowing down to get my bearings when a wolf jumped out of the grass, tearing wide circles in the dirt, my trap on its foot.

Merrill almost fell off behind me. This one could easily run off wearing the trap.

"Get that catchpole on it fast!" I angled the ATV away and we jumped off. I dug through my field kit, mixing Telazol and sterile water in a syringe as fast as I could. Instances like this taught me to always keep these three things in my shirt pocket when checking traps.

"Hurry, hurry," I said. I glanced over. I think I was talking to myself as much as to Merrill. The wolf was caught fast by its front toes. Merrill threw the catchpole loop around its neck and a cloud of dust went up in the struggle. For a moment, the two disappeared, but the wolf was down. I moved in with the needle. It all took less than two minutes.

I clapped Merrill on the shoulder.

"Now, aren't you glad you didn't stay in camp and cook breakfast?"

The Pinedale wolf was a collared female. I wondered if she might be from Yellowstone. I put her on the front seat of my truck, but first took a few photos of her with the herder, who grinned at getting to see a wolf up close. I didn't want to drug her twice unless I absolutely had to. Drugs are hard on wild animals. I had no way to secure her, so I tore my tent down as fast as I could and stuffed everything in the truck while Merrill phoned state biologists and asked to borrow a culvert trap. I drove the dozen or so miles to the end of the road where a small crew was waiting with a truck and the culvert trap on its trailer. It looked like a big sewer pipe with grating at one end. They helped me put the limp wolf inside and we hitched the whole thing to my truck. I found a phone in Pinedale and called Wayne Brewster, the head wildlife guy in Yellowstone. Bring her over, he said. We set up a place for me to rendezvous with rangers.

I grabbed a sandwich and began the long journey. My route took me through the middle of downtown Jackson Hole where cars and tourists plugged the road. People stared and tried to look in the culvert trap every time I stopped at a red light. When I made it to Yellowstone's south gate, the park ranger waved

*Robert, me and wolf Number 68 after her initial capture
in the Gros Ventre Wilderness, Wyoming.
(Collection of Carter Niemeyer)*

me through. Up the road, several biologists stood outside their trucks, waiting. A quick radio check confirmed it: This wolf was one of theirs. Number 68, a female. She was the first reintroduced wolf to have killed livestock in Wyoming.

Wayne wanted to put the wolf on the far side of Yellowstone Lake to discourage her from going south again, so we followed each other for miles past smiling, picnicking tourists. Nobody gave us a second glance. I backed my truck down a remote, closed road near a gravel pit, and when we were all positioned, we lifted the door. The wolf leapt out in a single bound and disappeared. Not so much as a limp.

I hoped she would stay in the park and stay out of trouble. But all I'd really done was to slow her down. She wasn't going to find what she wanted in Yellowstone.

A month later, Number 68 returned to the Gros Ventre, traveling more than 100 miles of rough, rocky country through other wolves' territories, and not just to eat sheep. She was reuniting with her boyfriend, the herd's Great Pyrenees guard dog. Merrill Nelson saw them hanging around together.

It wasn't the first time a wolf and a dog had paired up. In my career, I was aware of five of these incidents – three that involved puppies, which were quietly destroyed. The pattern was always the same: a female wolf and a male dog, and always around a livestock operation. Nobody usually notices except by accident. There normally isn't a human present to witness all the things that happen on a remote grazing allotment. In the case of the Gros Ventre sheep grounds, the herder was there, but apparently he never noticed the dog and the wolf together – unless he'd been trying to tell us by saying, "wolf-dog." The pairing had probably been established for a year or more, and whenever her estrus season came around, the wolf went to the sheep grounds to find her fellow. I realized that what I had heard the night Merrill and I camped wasn't the dog barking to alert the herder, but to communicate with his girlfriend. He had everybody fooled.

He probably was in on the killing, too. By the time it was over, Number 68 had killed upwards of 60 sheep. Merrill shot her at 2 a.m., one morning, in the act of killing more.

Maybe it sounds a little anthropomorphic, but Number 68 came from a bad family. I discovered much later that I had captured her before – as a pup – near Augusta, Montana. She and nine siblings were delivered from sure death in livestock country to the safety of Yellowstone, becoming known as the Sawtooth pack. They had come to Montana on their own, most likely from Canada. At one time, the pack totaled 18 members. The adults had been in trouble off and on for harassing and killing cattle on the L F Ranch. I surmised that having all those mouths to feed pushed the Sawtooth parents to prey on cattle, which they learned, don't know how to put up much of a fight. We tried various things to stop them: moving some wolves, killing some wolves, but in the end they wouldn't quit. That's pretty typical of livestock-killing wolves; it's almost impossible to get them to stop.

In the end, the ten half-grown puppies were all that remained. I climbed in a helicopter in August and September 1996 to dart them. We sent them in kennels to Yellowstone where biologists put them with two unrelated adult wolves in the park's Rose Creek pen. They weren't officially considered part of the rein-troduction, but brought the number of reintroduced wolves in the park to 41, which seemed like a good idea at the time. Biologists hoped they could be rehabilitated; beef was pretty much all they'd ever eaten.

The Sawtooths' story was mostly a sad one. After their release, they had virtually nothing to do with the adults in the pen. Five of Number 68's nine siblings left the park and were shot for killing sheep and cattle. One died after biting down on a sodium cyanide device, and another was killed by a car. The remaining two escaped further notoriety.

The pack's behavior was evidence that adult wolves are the teachers, and if cattle are what they kill, that's likely what the pups will kill. Their crimes are mostly those of opportunity. Most wolves don't bother livestock. But if elk and deer are in short supply – or people inadvertently lure them onto a ranch by leaving bone yards exposed – then wolves get comfortable taking a poke at calves and yearlings. More than once I've known ranchers who put bands of sheep totaling about 2,000 animals onto summer grazing ranges that were known wolf territories. When sheep started going down, the ranchers called the government and wanted the wolves killed. The rancher usually gets his way. The Sawtooth wolves got a couple of chances to change their ways in the days before territories were full and we could still find a place to release problem wolves. But things didn't work out because they were conditioned to killing cattle.

"In hindsight, it sounds like the idea sucked," Ed Bangs told the Jackson Hole News. "Children without a lot of parental supervision don't turn out that good."

Dogs or Wolves?

Sometimes wolves were guilty of killing livestock or committing other sins, like mating with guard dogs, but most of the time they were only guilty of hanging around. Wolves became victims of fear: They were in the neighborhood and something died, so it must be a wolf's fault. If a wolf was guilty, I was willing to say so, but I wasn't about to rubber stamp the claim of every rancher who lost a cow. I wanted evidence.

When an animal dies from something other than a predator attack, it looks like it simply fell over with its legs sticking straight out. If it's fevered, it may seek water. Prey that have been run down and killed by a wolf often go down on their sternums because the big leg and gluteus muscles that hold them up have been shredded. They don't curl up in a cozy spot along a trail. If you come upon a dead animal and you don't see torn up ground and predator tracks – really obvious signs that something traumatic happened – that animal may have died from something else. Check for a bullet. If livestock are simply missing, check for tire tracks. Vandalism and rustling are bigger problems for ranchers than most people think.

It is unusual for predators to kill prey and not consume it over a few days. They may leave it and come back rather than try to eat it all at once. Sometimes people disturb them or run them off, giving the impression that the wolf has killed it for no particular reason. Medicated prey often stays untouched by large carnivores. But that doesn't mean the bodies are wasted. The dead serve many, including scavenging mammals like coyotes, skunks and badgers as well as birds like magpies, ravens, eagles and vultures. Birds will often pick a carcass clean, but they don't fly off with large bones. Predators, on the other hand, often dismember their kills and carry away the parts.

I learned all of this because I spent so much time investigating dead livestock. The first thing I did wasn't to tromp all over the scene, but to ask the rancher by phone to cover up the carcass with a tarp and try to keep his dogs inside – and the neighbors away. When I got there, I went to the ranch house and often we had a cup of coffee and talked first. I tried not to be in a hurry to decide what had happened. I let them talk. I looked to see if the scene matched their story. Most of the ranchers I talked to were pretty good folks. Most of them didn't get too excited about the presence of wolves. They didn't care too much that I had helped out with the reintroduction. They were more interested in whether I knew what I was talking about.

I'll admit that at one time I was fairly intolerant of anything that rocked the rancher's world. I didn't know any better. My views evolved. I was proud of helping to bring wolves back and I wanted to see them get reestablished. I've always been for more wild things than fewer. What could it hurt, really? I knew that wolves were not responsible for all the livestock deaths that people reported because I investigated the scenes where the deaths occurred. Over the years, I have skinned out hundreds of cows, llamas, bulls, sheep, horses, you name it. Most die of something other than predator damage, but I'll admit that livestock dying from dehydration or from eating poisonous plants doesn't have the same ring to it. A predator – a wolf, especially – makes for a more exciting story. And sometimes it helps hide the responsibility of ranchers who didn't take care of their animals. Truth is just an irritating distraction.

What really surprises me is that things have never simmered down. I figured that, after reintroduction, people would climb off the ceiling and get used to wolves. I figured I'd go back to my old job and everything would go back to the way it was. Instead, wolves changed my life forever. It started when I was pressured to blame wolves whenever livestock was found dead. Being told what to think and what to write in my reports made my hackles go up. I wanted honesty, but some folks in my agency believed that ranchers should get everything they wanted, and wanted me to go along. No way. I couldn't believe I was getting crossways with people I'd worked with closely for more than twenty years. Wanting wolves to get a fair shake killed a lot of my friendships.

In more than one way, I knew where all the bodies were buried, and without really setting out to do it, my new interest became making sure that wolves and other predators didn't go down without someone fighting for them. I was tired of all of the needless death. I did a lot of the killing when I was a federal trapper, and I just got tired of it. It's bad for the soul.

On November 8, 1999, my phone rang in Helena. It was the state director, who said there was a dead calf near Polson, Montana, maybe a wolf kill. He asked me to help figure it out.

It happened in the mud, next to a reservoir, on the Flathead Reservation. Trappers Dave Nelson and Ted North took a look around and determined from the tracks that a wolf did the killing. They called the tribal game wardens and police. I learned that when they reported it to the head office, the Montana state director called and asked me to get involved.

I met Ted and Dave the next morning and we ate breakfast before heading to the reservation. This guy was one ornery old fart, Ted mumbled through his scrambled eggs.

When we pulled through the ranch gates, I recognized the place. I'd been here years ago when this fellow had coyote problems. Ted and Dave lingered in the driveway next to the trucks while I walked to the door and knocked.

"Well, I know you!" the man stepped out onto the porch and shook my hand. I was relieved he remembered me. "Come on in."

I motioned to my comrades. So much for the ornery rancher story.

The man gave us permission to do whatever we needed to do. He was positive that wolves were the villains, and he wanted them killed. We visited for a bit, then headed out to his acreage.

The calf was still there, lying in the mud on the reservoir's bank. We stepped all around it, carefully. Mud was the best thing you could hope for when looking for the tracks of the killer and subsequent visitors. All I saw were medium-size dog tracks.

Dave pointed at one of them. "There you go. Wolf."

He'd singled out a dog track where the animal had slipped in the mud, splaying the toes on one paw, making it appear larger.

"Yeah, but where are the others like it?" I countered. As far as I was concerned, the only canine that had visited this carcass was a dog.

The calf was slowly being eaten and it looked to me like a dog had fed on it that morning. I was pretty sure nothing killed it, but that it tipped over here at the water's edge, probably because it was sick. Dave and I went back and forth about the tracks and whether they belonged to wolves, but I said nothing else. I wanted to see what other evidence I could find. I looped my thumbs in my pockets and examined the ground away from the carcass, while Ted and Dave went off in the other direction.

I worked my way around the reservoir and followed a trail up-slope. I wasn't too far along when I encountered dog shit. Alpo, I thought. People always ask me the difference between

The guilty parties are tied to a log in an incident
that was nearly blamed on wolves.
(Photo by Carter Niemeyer)

wild and domestic canine shit. Commercial dog food forms a pale, mushy poop, but wild canines eat off the bone, which means their scat looks black, greasy and tapered, and it contains hair and bone fragments. I snapped on one latex glove and picked up the sample. I wanted my partners to see this. The dog's shit told me it was getting most of its meals out of a bowl somewhere and that the calf carcass was merely entertainment.

I crested the hill above the reservoir, but I could see several houses about a hundred yards away, so I angled through a stand of lodgepole pines and headed back toward the reservoir. I found another trail going my direction, so I took it. I wasn't twenty paces along when I met two big, black mutts.

I had startled them, and they barked and growled and bared their teeth. They looked like biters, so I faced them straight on and started talking softly. I crouched down and held the dog shit out in my hand. I was willing to bet it belonged to one of them. The dogs kept barking and cautiously sniffed the air. They finally calmed down a little, but I didn't trust them. One was wearing a collar. I was pretty sure these could be the ones eating the carcass. Why were they here, otherwise?

I made a wide circle around the dogs and continued toward the reservoir, keeping an eye on them over my shoulder. They followed me, barking and keeping their distance. I met Dave and Ted on the trail. They'd heard the noise and were coming to investigate.

"Turn around and walk with me," I said, and kept going. I wanted to see if the dogs would follow. We went left and the dogs went right – directly to the calf carcass.

"I think we just solved the mystery," I whispered to Dave. He nodded. He was seeing it with his own eyes.

Ted owned hounds and I knew he might have a sack of dog food in his truck. How about a leash? He had that, too.

I went alone toward the dogs and sat down on a log about fifty feet away. I rustled the food sack and threw a small handful towards them. The collared one approached me, hackles up, but ate everything I'd thrown out. The collared dog was tantalized, as are most dogs, by any kind of new food, and the delicious sound of crinkling paper. They were probably pets that were simply allowed to run at large; at least that's how they acted. I offered more food and the dog came to my outstretched hand. The other dog was wilder and kept chewing on the calf, but the collared one relaxed and let me touch its head. It seemed ravenous. I gave it more food and petted its head slowly, moving my hand down its neck until I got to the collar. Then I moved in with the leash in my other hand and snapped it on the collar's ring. The dog suddenly realized what was happening and struggled, but didn't try to bite me. I tied him to the log and tossed him another handful of food to keep him quiet. Then I stood and walked back to my truck.

Dave and Ted stood in front of their trucks watching all of this. I retrieved a wolf neck snare from the bed of my pickup and headed back toward the carcass. The snare was a souvenir from the wolf capture days in Canada. It had a metal stop clamped on part of the cable that kept it from cinching all the way down and strangling the animal.

The un-collared dog paced back and forth at a distance and watched me. It seemed to want the food I offered, but was skittish. This next part was a long shot, I thought. I looped the ten-foot long snare around the log and opened the loop on the other end. It took awhile, but the un-collared dog slowly let its guard down. It watched me pet its buddy and decided to give the dog food a try. It inched closer and closer. I reached my hand toward the dog as slowly as I could and touched it. It jumped away, but then returned, and that's when I slipped the snare over its neck and jerked tight.

The dog went berserk, flipping and pulling and floundering. It yelped frantically, but could not escape. I jumped up and ran back to my truck, motioning the guys to pile in with me. The rancher wasn't too surprised when I broke the news to him. He'd forgotten that he'd seen a couple of dogs running around his pasture recently.

We called the tribal police and led them to the dogs, which they took away. I knew that finding the guilty dogs wouldn't help me with the folks who always wanted to blame wolves, but I felt that the evidence was clear. This time, wolves were off the hook.

Chasing Crystals

The vast and magnificent Lamar Valley kept popping in and out of my life, or more precisely, I seemed to be making periodic, unplanned pilgrimages to it, inserted into the capture and collaring of wolves wherever and whenever I was needed.

The valley is the deepest part of the heart of Yellowstone, which is perhaps why biologists decided to put the wolves there. I'd been there on a different mission in 1975, many moons before wolves ever crossed my mind, climbing part way up Soda Butte to release golden eagles. The huge birds were regularly killing lambs near Dillon, Montana, about 100 miles away. The release in Lamar Valley seemed like a good idea on paper, but many of the eagles returned to the sheep allotment and kept on killing.

In later years, I returned to the valley because of the Rose Creek wolves. And in the years after that, I was there, darting from a helicopter to help capture and collar wolves in other packs, including the formidable Druid wolves, known worldwide as the largest pack ever recorded in North America – 37 animals. I once crested a ridge in winter in the chopper to see almost all of the Druids fanned out in front of me, running across their brilliant land of snow.

I've never tired of seeing Lamar Valley from a helicopter. We flew without doors for practical reasons, but it made me feel closer to the place. In 1998, I saw the valley from the air for the first time when I went there to help capture wolves in the Crystal Creek pack to replace their radio collars. It was the first time anyone had tried to dart wolves from a helicopter in Yellowstone.

The Crystal Creek wolves lived in Lamar Valley chiefly because they were habituated to the park after being released from the Crystal Creek pen, one of the five pens scattered throughout remote parts of Yellowstone. They weren't fighters like the Druid wolves. Wolves kill each other fairly often, usually in disputes about territories, and some packs are bigger fighters than others. Only humans cause more wolf deaths. Wolves are fierce about their territories because that is where they hunt and raise their young. They have no choice. In their world, it's kill or be killed, although there are confounding instances where lone wolves will break away from the pack and travel great distances to find a mate or another family.

The original breeding pair of the Crystal Creek pack included the male, Number 4, and female, Number 5. When the Druids invaded the valley, they killed Number 4, and possibly a den full of puppies. Number 5 led the pack away, eventually settling twenty or so miles away, in Yellowstone's Pelican Valley. By 1996, the pack was down to two, Number 5 and Number 6, an unrelated male that had been part of the pack since reintroduction. He had become her new mate.

The Crystal Creek wolves were remarkable for a number of reasons, including making themselves regularly visible to tourists. Time made another reason stand out: Of all of the wolves and packs in Yellowstone, the Crystal Creek and the Delta wolves are the only two family bloodlines that have continued uninterrupted since they were turned out into the park in 1995.

Wolves in the Crystal Creek pack pace the pen before their release into Yellowstone National Park.
(Photo courtesy Yellowstone National Park)

Yellowstone's chief wolf expert, Doug Smith, attributes the unity of the Crystal Creek wolves to low breeder turnover in the pack, and the early establishment of a territory in a fairly isolated part of the park.

Researchers can't continue to know and study any of this unless radio collars work, and by 1998, the collars of the Crystal Creek pair, Number 5 and Number 6, were failing, and the puppies that had been born in 1997 were not collared yet.

A capture team from New Zealand thought it might be easy to catch the wolves by using a net gun. They'd been all over the world net-gunning wildlife for research purposes and figured Yellowstone would be a cinch. They were wrong. The wolves preferred heavily timbered areas and the trees kept the Kiwi capture team from getting close. After that, park officials worried that messing up with high-profile wolves would give Yellowstone a black eye. By then, I had 45 captures under my belt, so when Doug called me, I said yes.

We set up at dawn at the Gardiner, Montana, airstrip, just outside Yellowstone's famous stone-arched north entrance, to settle on a number of details. Doug wondered if it was OK if Dr. Dave Mech flew with me. He was there on other business, but wanted to get in on some fieldwork. My jaw dropped. Dave is a chief scientist for the U.S. Geological Survey, and has written major textbooks on wolf biology and behavior. We called him "The Godfather." Did I mind? I was elated. I hadn't seen him since reintroduction three years earlier when we knelt on the floor together tending to wolves in Canada. Besides wolves, we had talked about mink trapping and the Midwest. Dave is old school, a hunter and hobby trapper, and a no-nonsense guy when it comes to wolves. He might have been world famous, but he was a Midwest kid at heart. Kerry Murphy, another biologist, was my other handler. We flew with Gary Brennan, a superb helicopter pilot.

When I first flew with Gary, before we ever chased down a wolf, we had to learn a little bit about each other's roles in the chopper. I would pick out a bush or a clump of grass as a target and have him hover us about 30 feet away. That was the shooting angle I wanted when we were in pursuit, I said. On dry ground, wolves can run at speeds up to 35 mph., so we worked in snow. Deep snow, preferably. It slowed down the animal and increased my odds of having to spend only one or two darts to drug it. In turn, Gary gave me a primer on the physics of rotor wash – the wind generated by the helicopter's blades – and showed me how to keep my lightweight, aluminum dart speeding in the direction I fired it, despite the forces working against me.

On this day, conditions were perfect. Brennan ferried us in his Hughes 500 to Pelican Valley, where the wolves had been seen most recently. Above us, Roger Stradley flew spotter in his yellow Supercub as he has for thousands of hours for the park. Doug climbed in with Roger and helped keep track of the wolves we chased. It wasn't long before there was action.

We found an area where bison had packed down the snow, and let Dave and Kerry out. The giant animals moved away, breathing out white vapor in the cold. We hoped to return shortly with wolves. Gary and I unfastened the chopper's doors and laid them in the snow. We would be doing fast and stressful maneuvers, which meant the chopper needed to be as light as possible. We lifted into the sky and saw the pack almost immediately. I pushed a dart into my gun. I'd been holding it tight in my hand to keep the contents from freezing. I had 14 more in my parka, keeping them warm.

Ahead of us, in the brilliant blue and white landscape, were pine trees. Lots of them. The Crystal Creek wolves were headed there full blast. The big male, Number 6, was black, and his mate, Number 5, was a grayish-peach tone. Three others, yearlings, ran with them. I could understand why the New Zealand crew couldn't catch these wolves. Too many trees to deploy a net gun. It would tangle in the branches and miss the animals. Gary raced us toward them.

"Are you ready?" His voice was strong in my headset. He'd been on plenty of high-velocity animal captures and flew his chopper like a combat pilot, zipping suddenly sideways, suddenly down. I nodded, pointing my dart gun out the open side of the chopper, bracing one leg on the door frame and leaning into my harness. I waited for wolves to appear below me.

Gary chased the wolves, and they bounded through chest-deep snow. His strategy was to push them into the circular openings made by small, seasonal ponds. They were only about 100 yards across. Gary swooped side to side, herding them, trying to keep them in a group for me. Then the pack split. He went after Number 6, but the wolf skirted the openings, staying in the trees. Then Number 6 made a run for it, and Gary was on him, getting down within twenty feet. I fired.

The dart sank neatly into black fur at the hip and Gary pulled up hard and circled, like a carnival ride. Then he hovered and flew to the side of the wolf, keeping it in the open until it stood still in the deep snow, finally going limp from the drugs, its head resting upright.

We landed away from the wolf, unbuckled ourselves and climbed out. Gary brought out his video camera. I made my way toward the wolf, sinking hip-deep. The closer I got, the bigger the wolf looked. I could see that his abdomen was bulging from a recent meal. I grabbed him by the scruff and the fur on his back and tried to pull him along, but I sank deeper and the wolf didn't move. I motioned to Gary that I needed help. By the time we wrestled this one into the chopper, we were exhausted.

But there was no time to catch our breath. Roger and Doug had spotted Number 5. She was where we could get to her.

"Be really careful," Doug radioed. "She's probably pregnant."

Gary worked her into a snowless, steaming, gravel bed. I pulled the hammer back on the dart gun and took aim. But the wolf dove into deep snow and disappeared. Gary circled back, but she was gone. We went around again. No wolf. We hovered and talked through our headsets. She must have jumped into a den.

Gary set us down in the gravel while we decided what to do. The big male lay in the chopper's back seat, his tongue hanging lazily out of his mouth, his eyes blinking. He'd be like this for about a half hour, so we let the helicopter idle there and hiked the 150 feet to the last place we had seen Number 5's tracks. They led to a cavern, but I couldn't tell how deep or extensive it was. She could disappear farther into it, or less likely, feel cornered and lunge at us. We hoped she would be docile because the deep snow would keep us from moving fast.

On closer inspection, I could see that Number 5's haven was actually formed by a root of an enormous fallen tree. I got down on my knees and peered inside, my eyes adjusting from the blinding glare of snow. Then I saw a pair of hairy legs. She was sitting upright inches in front of me, her head obscured in a tangle of roots. I can't see you, so you can't see me, I'm pretty sure she was thinking. I was too close to risk a shot with the dart gun so I retreated quietly and used first-aid tape to attach a loaded syringe onto a slender lodgepole branch. I lay on my belly and inched forward into the cavern. The wolf didn't move. I pushed the needle toward her shoulder. She still didn't move. So I pushed the needle into her. She remained unphased. Gary stopped filming and looked at his watch to mark the time. We waited for the drug to kick in – about ten minutes. Only then did I climb part way into the hole and poke at her slightly. She was out, still sitting upright. I pulled on her leg and she collapsed on my arm. I could see she was, indeed, full of pups. I slid her out of her hiding place. Soon we had her loaded and headed back.

Dr. Dave Mech, me and two Crystal Creek pack wolves. At the time the
dark wolf was the largest wolf ever captured in Yellowstone.
(Collection of Carter Niemeyer)

Dave and Kerry were dots in the vast white. We descended straight toward them and they covered their faces from the whirl of glistening powder.

I had handled a lot of wolves but I had never lifted a wolf the size of Number 6. We placed the still-drugged, black wolf onto a canvas cloth attached at four corners to a spring scale. Kerry and I lifted the enveloped wolf, scale and all, and Dave crouched, reading the number while Gary recorded it all on videotape.

"One hundred and...forty one," Dave said, writing it on the data sheet. We let the wolf down with a grunt.

It was the biggest wolf captured in the Northern Rockies recovery area.

Number 5 tipped the scales at 115 pounds. She had weighed a respectable 95 pounds when she was brought to Yellowstone from Canada. Then, after their release, the Crystal Creek pack learned to kill bison. They were the only wolves we knew of to do it regularly. Both Number 5 and Number 6 appeared to have a gut filled with meat the day we captured them, maybe 10-15 pounds each. Genetics can do a certain amount, but from what I've encountered, size has a lot to do with nutrition. These wolves were big because they had a hefty supply of food.

When we were done poking and measuring, we carried the two wolves to the tree line and used our boots to hollow out a couple of snow drifts. We pushed the wolves inside. They were almost alert now, but until they had their wits about them, their little snow cave would provide safety in case bison approached. The animals seemed to like this area because of the steam vents. By the time we packed our gear into the helicopter, the wolves were up and moving.

But we weren't done yet.

The Crystal Creek pack yearlings had no collars, which was going to make them difficult to follow. Roger and Doug flew and found them the next morning, guiding us from their higher vantage point. The pack of five had reunited nearby. Doug knew that six pups had been born the previous year. He'd seen them from the air. But now only three were with the pack.

Soon we were on them, chasing a gray yearling. I fired a dart, but saw it glance off the animal's hip. I reloaded and we were pulling around fast to try again when the wolf tipped over. The only thing I could figure was that I'd hit an artery and mainlined the Telazol. I'd never seen anything like it. The wolf lay in the middle of a steaming bed of gravel and snow – quintessential Yellowstone scenery. The commotion of us landing jarred the wolf and it struggled to get up. Maybe it didn't get a full dose, or maybe it was metabolizing it with lightning speed. I quickly gave it a liberal dose of Ketamine. It was going to take time to capture the others and I had to make sure this one was completely immobilized and wouldn't bite me or thrash around once it was loaded into the chopper, possibly launching itself out the door.

It's not easy to wrestle the dead weight of a 100-pound, or more, wolf into the back of a helicopter. This one, we found later, weighed 115 pounds, just like his mother. The door was above elbow-height for me, and I'm pretty tall. This meant I had to get the wolf almost up to my shoulders to put it on the floor of the chopper. It was more of a heave ho, flopping it through the door. Sometimes they didn't land right. A few times I had to move quickly to make sure a wolf's airway wasn't kinked when the limp animal landed mostly on its head.

Next up was a black wolf and I spent two darts trying to get it. Gary used the chopper to direct the wolf along a snowy ridge once it was hit, keeping it in the open so we could land and retrieve it. His expertise at the controls of a helicopter was amazing, and made my job easier. Ahead was one more black wolf. Gary swooped down, intercepting it in a small opening between trees, and I put a dart in its butt. This one wandered downhill and lay down next to a swamp. I couldn't tell if its face was in the water. I motioned to Gary.

"We gotta get down there quick."

Gary dropped us toward land but kept the ship in a hover, inches from the muck, right next to the drugged wolf.

I unbuckled, took off my helmet and put my foot out on one skid. The wolf was only about six feet away. I took one step toward it and sank to my knee. I hung on to the helicopter for fear I would go into the swamp and never come out. I pulled my leg back and the muck let go of me. I yelled at Gary that I was having problems and to keep the ship right there if he could. The strain of the helicopter's engine was deafening. I tried again, but this time I stayed on the skid and worked my way toward the wolf, as close as I could get. I put a foot into the swamp again and grabbed for the wolf all in one motion. I pulled the animal toward me and summoned all my strength to get it and myself onto the helicopter skid. All I did was move it a little closer. With one more try, I had it out of the swamp. I inched back toward the door with the wolf, like I was on a balance beam. Gary couldn't see all of this and later said he wondered what the hell I was doing as he felt the ship rocking to and fro.

With three wolves asleep in the back seat, I climbed back in with Gary for the trip down to the awaiting processing team. I smelled like rotten eggs because of the sulfur-rich swamp water, another feature of Yellowstone. We weighed and collared them, and returned them to the area where I had darted them. When they awoke, they probably wondered what had happened.

In August 1998, many months after we captured the Crystal Creek wolves, the breeding male of the pack, Number 6, was found dead near a bull elk carcass. Number 6, the biggest wolf in Yellowstone, had bled to death, most likely. His femoral artery was severely damaged. Scientists pieced together the evidence at the scene and guessed that the wolf's wound had been caused by an antler – maybe belonging to the elk that lay there. Their other theory was that a grizzly bear wanted the elk meat and fought the wolf for it.

In 2000, Yellowstone officials renamed the Crystal Creek pack. From then on, the wolves became known as Mollie's Pack, after the late Mollie Beattie, director of the U.S. Fish and Wildlife Service during reintroduction. She died of cancer in 1996, but had done a lot in her short life, including being the first woman to run the agency.

At this writing, Mollie's Pack is still out there.

Trap Signs

In the early days after wolf reintroduction, I seldom used trap signs. I didn't need to. In the 1990s, there was hardly a soul wandering around out where I trapped in remote parts of Montana. Then, a few at a time, people started showing up, setting up camp and sometimes blowing wolves out of the neighborhood. When ATVs became popular, it got worse. It was maddening. Wolf researchers trapped primarily on federal land, which is nearly the only place left in the West for the wolf. But these places are required to be almost everything to almost everyone. That meant we had a hard time over the years in the delicate waltz of using steel traps in areas where people could set them off. As a result, the wolf team – a handful of biologists from the U.S. Fish and Wildlife Service and the Nez Perce Tribe, which took on the task of monitoring wolves when the State of Idaho forbade its fish and game agency from participating – decided to start using trap signs. At first, people read them and went the other way. Then they quit obliging me. It's hard to say who was right. They had a right to be there, but their presence sure created problems.

I printed the signs in my office on a big fancy copy machine, often jamming it and needing the help of tech-savvy coworkers who usually rolled their eyes. The signs had small type with a bunch of information about avoiding the area, phone numbers and a federal emblem. Later, the signs had an official-looking color emblem and the silhouette of a wolf, with fewer words and larger print. Even later, I put them on fluorescent paper. People still ignored them, or sometimes stole them or wrote derogatory comments on the sign's laminated coating. I started putting up half a dozen signs, warning that dogs could easily get caught. I hung them low, over the middle of the road, suspended by a tree limb, so that people had no choice but to let the sign drape lazily across their windshields as they passed into the area where my traps lay in wait.

The ones who saw my signs, shrugged and continued on (as I imagine it), were often the same folks who had to go to some effort to get around large metal U.S. Forest Service gates with signs in big, block letters: Road Closed. I had permission from the ranger to be in there, and I'd picked that spot because the wolves left evidence that they'd been using the road. It was even better that the road turned out to be closed because of other reasons like fire danger or vandalism. So it baffled me to be six miles up there, hacking away at hard earth, making a spot for a trap, and have people come by on horseback and tip their hats, three or four dogs trailing behind them.

I escaped Wildlife Services in Montana, in 2000, by taking a new job in Boise, Idaho: the wolf recovery coordinator for the U.S. Fish and Wildlife Service. My job was to do whatever I needed to do to get people and wolves to get along. In Idaho, mine was the final say.

While my new bosses would have liked me to stay in my swivel chair and answer phone calls and write reports, I grabbed every chance to be outdoors – in particular putting collars on wolves. After all, I was a trapper. Dirt and grime and a good sunburn came first.

So I eagerly accepted when biologists from the Nez Perce Tribe invited me to accompany them on a trapping gig. Curt Mack ran the tribe's wolf program, which mostly involved federal lands on Idaho's west side. But with only a few biologists and me to help, we had a lot of ground to cover in the backcountry. State biologists couldn't touch wolf monitoring; it was a way for the state to take an anti-federal stand and protest reintroduction. On this August weekend, Mack wanted to trap a member of the Landmark pack, a group of twelve grays that wandered in and out of the Frank Church-River of No Return Wilderness. Only one radio collar functioned in the pack and its battery was dying. If we didn't replace it soon, we'd lose track of these wolves.

We met at a restaurant in Stanley and I was dismayed to hear they'd already set traps. I was hoping to get in on the scouting. We spread a map on the table and biologists Adam Gall and Jason Husseman pointed to a place northwest of town called Seafoam. Telemetry readings showed the wolves were close to that area, so that's where the guys set traps. All I could do was be a helper at this point. Still, I wanted to see the area they'd chosen.

We headed down the highway and turned off into the hills. It was Friday, and I noted with a slight twinge, that traffic had gotten thicker ever since we had left the main road. We passed tents, people building campfires, strings of tethered horses, dogs chasing each other, kids chasing dogs. There was even a car overturned in a ditch, probably the result of a good party. A mile or so farther up, slightly past an area where several dozen trailers were parked every which way, was the trap line. A couple of motocross bikes went ripping by, leaving a blinding cloud of dust. We stopped and got out. Curt pointed at the orange tape on a tree branch, indicating a trap was close by.

We meandered around and waited for each other to say something. So I did.

"You guys need to pull all of these," I said, trying not to sound like a jerk. "What will you do if you catch more than one wolf? I could picture the circus in my head. Trapping for wolves along roads and trails was standard because when it came to steep terrain wolves preferred paths of least resistance, but usually we trapped only when there wasn't a sign of a human for miles.

"I'd pick one spot and just trap there until all these people leave." I tried to sound like I was making a suggestion rather than bossing them around. It was their trap line not mine, but the buck stopped with me if there was a problem.

They agreed and we started the dusty task of snapping traps and throwing them in the back of the pickup. We dilly-dallied when people drove by, trying not to be obvious about what we were doing. I knew the guys were probably pissed. Setting that many traps takes a lot of work. When we headed toward the final string of traps set along Winnemucca Trail, Curt argued his case.

"The wolves just left these tracks," he said.

I agreed. The trail was used mainly by ATV riders; people seldom walked it. We posted a sign at the trailhead: Warning! Wolf Traps In Area!

This might have been a good time to abandon the tribal biologists. After all, they were asking for trouble. But Jenny Valdivia from the U.S. Fish and Wildlife Service's regional office in Portland was traveling to Idaho with the express purpose

Would you take your dogs up this road?
(Photo by Carter Niemeyer)

of trying to get a glimpse of wolves. Jenny was a public affairs officer and would later become my wife. She was bringing a friend, Sue Burkhart-Kasch. They usually went bird watching, but wolves sounded pretty exciting. I wanted to produce something for them. Trying to collar the Landmark pack seemed like the perfect field trip.

Saturday morning, I was back at home in Boise, waiting for my guests. Jenny had called the night before, asking what time they should be at my house.

"I think 4:30 a.m. would be good," I said.

Silence.

"Really?" she said.

"Or 3:30. Unless that's too early." I wondered if she had a sense of humor.

"Well, uh...okay...."

"Naw, 7:30 is fine," I said. She laughed a little.

She and Sue showed up right on time the next morning, just as I was setting the sprinkler on my parched yard. I'd bought a house but it looked an awful lot like nobody lived in it. We drove off, three across in my pickup, and Sue produced donuts and coffee.

"Do you drink coffee?" Jenny asked.

"Nothing ceremonial," I said. She looked at me, then tipped her thermos and poured coffee in my cup.

"What the hell does that mean?" she laughed.

Curt Mack turned over his trapping duties to Jason Husseman, and on Saturday morning, Jason and Adam flew with local pilot Bob Danner to find the Landmark wolves. Telemetry signals took them to a side drainage of Bear Creek, a short distance from the trap line. Jenny, Sue and I ate breakfast in Stanley and waited for Jason and Adam to show up. Then all of us convoyed for about 25 miles to the base of a small mountain. If we were sneaky, we might see the Landmark wolves.

It was hot, and the hill we hiked was steep, brushy and trailless. The worst part was that every time we crested, there was another peak to conquer. Jason and Adam took off like gazelles. The rest of us plodded along and talked about the wildflowers we were seeing and about wolves. I'd taken along a dart gun and my ghillie suit – a sort of Sasquatch camouflage ensemble. I thought I might get a chance to dart and collar a wolf if we happened upon them. Finally, we reached the top. It had only been a mile, but seemed like ten.

Sue had the best pair of binoculars, and I kept borrowing them. My telemetry receiver was pinging away full tilt. The wolves were very close. I looked down into the wet meadow a thousand yards away. Somebody commented on the chunks of cottonwood strewn around the stream.

"One of your cottonwood logs just moved," I said. I was looking right at them through the binoculars.

It was the Landmarks. All twelve of them. They were napping in the sunny meadow, occasionally raising their heads, or lazily getting up to lap at the stream before plopping back down next to another pack member. We took turns looking through Sue's binoculars. I suggested that Jason, Adam and I look for the route down the mountain that the wolves were taking. It would make trapping a lot easier. I told Jenny and Sue to stay up on top as long as they wanted, just go downhill to the east and they'd run into the road. I'd find them, I said.

They looked at each other, unsure, then nodded.

As it happened, once they put away their binoculars and left the mountain, no one ever saw the entire pack again.

The sun was setting, and I'd been off the mountain for about a half hour. All I saw was horse tracks on my way down. I figured Jason and Adam were still at it. I ate a sandwich in my truck, parked off the side of the road. Jenny and Sue should appear at any time.

Then something in my driver's side mirror caught my eye. A man and woman on horseback were making their way up to me. They paused and looked at my federal plates and said something to each other. Three small dogs came racing up with them. Great, I mumbled. I rolled down my window.

"Are you with the wolf program?" the woman asked. She didn't seem like she was in a very good mood.

"Yes...." I started.

"Did you know you caught our 13-year-old dog in one of your traps?"

Now she was almost yelling.

"How does that make you feel, to catch an old dog in a trap like that?"

I was starting to explain that no, those were not my personal wolf traps, but yes, I was with the people trapping, but she didn't care. Why would she? Her husband dismounted and pulled a trap out of his saddlebag. It was the tribe's.

I looked at the beagle they said had been caught. He looked unhurt. He wasn't even limping. I introduced myself, but I wasn't sure they were even listening.

"When did all this happen?" I asked.

"An hour ago! We let him out of the trap! Does that make you feel like a man?" She went on about knowing Gov. Dirk Kempthorne and how she was going to have my job and that I'd be hearing from the governor, and on and on. The dogs sniffed around the road and acted like nothing exciting had happened all day.

She can have my job, I wanted to tell her.

The husband, who had said little, shoved the trap back in his saddlebag and got on his horse, and they and their dogs kept going down the road.

I started my truck and made a U-turn. I should have put a stop to all the trapping when I could. Then Adam rounded the corner in his truck. Our windows met and I relayed what had just happened.

"Take my ATV and go. I want every goddamn one of those traps pulled now." I pulled open the tailgate of my truck and we unloaded the machine.

"Meet us at The Mountain Village," I said as Adam bolted away. He looked a little stunned. It was going to take him a couple of hours, and by then it would be dark.

Now I needed to find everybody else. How did a day that started out pretty nice turn into such a mess?

I cruised the dusty road back and forth a few times and finally saw Jenny and Sue come off an old, overgrown Forest Service trail. They climbed in, cheerful and chattering. The wolves never did move much from their spot in the meadow, they reported. I told them about the unfolding drama as I made another U-turn and headed south, where I expected Jason to be. He sat ahead on the side of the road.

"I saw some tracks, but nothing fresh," he started, all four of us wedged in the front seat of the truck.

"I just got my ass chewed over a dog getting trapped up the road," I said. I re-enacted the entire episode for my small audience, ending with the abrupt order I'd just barked at Adam.

Family shoots dog stuck in wolf trap in recreation area

Biologists place traps along trails wolves travel on

By Pete Zimowsky
The Idaho Statesman

A Kuna family's pet dog was put out of its misery after it stepped in a wolf trap Saturday in a popular recreation area near Stanley.

The incident now has the U.S. Fish and Wildlife Service rethinking its wolf-trapping program in areas where recreationists are concentrated.

"Sammy was behind us, and I heard this terrible screech," said Mindy Youngman, who recalled the incident Monday at her home.

"She was screeching and biting. I tried to pull the trap off her leg," she said. "At this point, I was freaking out."

Youngman, and her husband, Philip, and son, Noah, were camped near the Winnemucca Trail, in the Capehorn/Seafoam area, about 25

The Idaho Statesman newspaper ran the story of Sammy's demise on its front page.

We talked about it all the way to the restaurant. We sat down at 9 p.m. The sky was purple, revealing a sliver of moon in the west.

Spaghetti and meatballs sounded pretty good, and that's what we all ate. I was just finishing when the door opened and Adam came in, dirty, sweaty and looking unhappier than the last time I'd seen him.

"Well," he approached the table and shoved his hands in his pockets, "I just helped some people bury their dog."

"Really." I leaned back in my chair. I guess the day could get worse.

"The guy shot his dog. Can you believe that? He shot his fuckin' dog because it got in a trap."

Adam stood there for a second, then plopped down in a chair, and drank one of the waters that hadn't been touched. The waitress asked if he wanted food. He waved her away.

"I was just coming around the corner and it had just happened. I heard it from down the road. I could have pulled that trap if it had been just a couple minutes later," he said, getting angrier the more he talked.

The married couple, their toddler son, and their white shepherd dog, Sammy, from Kuna, Idaho, were camping beside the tree that had one of our wolf signs wired to it. If they had read it, they purposely ignored the warning, and walked with their dog unleashed up Winnemucca Trail. They passed two wolf traps set at the edge of the road, invisible under a fine sifting of dirt. It wasn't until they were on the way back that Sammy was lured in, the way a wolf would be, by the fetid bait, and the trap snapped on a front paw.

According to the wife, the dog began screeching in pain, and neither she nor her husband were able to collect their thoughts and remove the trap, so the husband pulled out his handgun and shot it. Newspapers and television stations ran the story for a week.

In more than 40 years of trapping, I'd never heard of such a thing. Who would shoot a dog instead of trying to rescue it?

Adam rubbed his face and looked at the floor. I wondered if this incident would sour him on wolf work.

"I'm sorry, man," I said, shaking his shoulder. "You guys don't need to deal with anybody on this. Send calls to me if you get them." I knew it would be a matter of hours before the newspapers started calling. I was responsible, even if they weren't my traps.

I drove Jenny and Sue back to Boise. I still couldn't believe what had happened. Once back in town, I wanted to get a jump on the mayhem, so I went to the office early on Sunday and wrote a detailed report. I hadn't been in my office long when the Idaho Statesman called. The story about Sammy landed on the front page above the fold the next morning, a little photo of the smiling dog right in the middle. From there, television picked it up, the governor's office called, and generally, all hell broke loose for about a week.

Two weeks after the incident, I had visitors in the lobby. The guard called me down and I met the folks who had been on horseback. They handed me the trap and said they'd had enough of the circus surrounding the whole dog-shooting incident. They just wanted it to go away. I agreed. Mistakes, all the way around, that's all this was about.

Sammy may have died, but the story was alive and kicking for a long time. The following summer, I received a letter postmarked The White House. It was typed on heavy, expensive paper, and was signed at the bottom by President George W. Bush. From all the markings and stamps and initials on it, the letter appeared to have worked its way through the intestines of the Department of the Interior and was finally plopped unceremoniously on my desk. It demanded a full explanation of how

Sammy had met his maker. Pretty fast, I remember typing. I tried to be as professional as I could as I sat writing back to the President. I added that the whole thing could have been avoided if Sammy's family had only heeded the trap sign.

The Avery Wolves

The trail to Bronson Meadows was the worst one I'd ever seen.

"We're gonna ride down that?" I pointed.

Dave Spicer, Josh Stanley and I unloaded our ATVs, readied field gear and sat astride our idling bikes. The trail before us, in the extreme backcountry, looked like a cliff: straight downhill on a roadbed shaped like a V. We descended slowly, our tires riding on the outsides of their rubber. At times, we balanced on two wheels. It was mid-June 2005. We were after wolves near Avery, a tiny town of fewer than 30 residents in northern Idaho.

Dave was the head Idaho Fish and Game biologist for the area, and Josh was a conservation officer – the modern day name for a game warden. They were wildlife professionals, eager to be involved in wolf management and conservation.

At the time, wolves were on the verge of being removed from federal protection in Idaho. Their numbers had swelled to 512 by 2005, and residents of northern Idaho had been calling the fish and game office, saying they'd seen wolves. Dave called me for help trapping and getting a collar in this group of wolves. It was the way the state kept track of their numbers. It wasn't the state's idea; it was a permanent federal requirement.

I wanted to be there, but the timing couldn't have been worse. I'd already taken any chance to get out from behind my desk in Boise, and had just set traps for what was possibly a new wolf pack in central Idaho near the Lochsa River, in wild, forested country east of the Nez Perce reservation. I dithered about what to do. I was particular when it came to trapping and didn't like to turn things over to just anyone, but I also wanted to help Dave. I gave in to the new chase and left my Lochsa trap line to Nez Perce biologist Isaac Babcock and his team. I had faith in Isaac. If the wolves were there, he wouldn't scare them off.

I drove north and now faced an ATV ride from hell into Bronson Meadows in order to get reasonably close to the wolves.

I usually pay close attention to the weather in the mountains, but today I was distracted by the ride. I didn't much notice the monstrous thunderheads rising in the west. We zigzagged our way slowly for several miles down the mountain. Bushes and branches clawed at us, and several times we each nearly went over our handlebars. A dozen times, I was at a standstill as I pivoted on two wheels to keep from tipping over. By the time we got to the bottom, I only vaguely noticed thunder rumbling. I was busy wondering where I might set traps, happy that I hadn't flown off the ATV and busted my head – or worse, spilled my traps down the canyon. I dreaded the idea of motoring back up that road.

We followed a trail to the east, which wound through thick willows and crisscrossing creeks. The fine silt preserved wolf tracks perfectly, and the ones we saw were fresh. This was a corridor, and it was where I would set traps. I spent the next couple of hours putting four traps in the ground. My cohorts watched from their machines. I'd asked them not to get off or walk around, or spit or pee anywhere near the trap line. I was kind of picky. In the past, it had caused some to roll their eyes, but I usually had a catch to show for all my work.

We turned around and went west, riding slowly right through what turned out to be the wolves' rendezvous site. This was the place they gathered, rested and reunited – a wolf living room of sorts. Scattered throughout the grassy resting area were plastic jugs, beer cans and a pair of shed moose antlers, all with tiny punctures made by puppy teeth. These were the pups' toys, brought home by the adults. Over the years, I've encountered orange highway cones, a logger's boot, bear skulls, plastic bottles and lots of beer cans in rendezvous sites. I usually stop and examine oddball items I see along a road in wolf country. Often they have teeth marks, evidence of wolf pups somewhere in the vicinity.

But I didn't want to catch puppies. In mid-June they would be about eight weeks old and much too small to collar safely. A pup will outgrow its collar quickly and can slowly asphyxiate. The collars, screwed together with brass fittings, don't stretch and are designed for adults. Some researchers try to fudge the fit with foam padding that is supposed to fall out when a pup grows, but usually the collar falls off shortly after collaring or the pup eventually chokes to death, slowly. I won't put a radio collar on a wolf pup that doesn't weigh at least 50 pounds.

We motored about a half-mile past the rendezvous site and I set five more traps. Each was attached to a drag – an eight-foot chain with a hook on the end to keep the wolf from running too far with the trap on its foot before the drag tangled in the underbrush. I dug a small hole that looked like a ground squirrel burrow and put a glob of irresistibly stinky lure deep inside. On the front side of the hole, I concealed my trap and drag with fine dirt. When the wolf went to sniffing around the hole and began stepping madly to get at the stinky lure, it would inevitably step in the trap – usually with its front foot.

It was late afternoon when we headed back up the mountain. The ride out was easier than the ride in, but now lightning crackled across the sky. My gut knotted. Our trap line was about to be ruined. Why wasn't I paying attention to the weather? I cussed myself. We stashed our ATVs in the dense forest brush rather than load them in the trucks again. By the time we pulled away from the trailhead, fat raindrops were hitting the windshield.

Josh Stanley invited me to stay the night at his home in nearby Silverton. He made supper while I unloaded gear from my truck. It was flat out raining now and I was glad not to be camping out. But I was getting that sinking feeling: My traps were probably lying in puddles, useless because they were no longer concealed. In the morning, when it was still dark, we gobbled some breakfast before heading out. I wanted to be checking traps at first light.

"You have a creek behind your place?" I asked between mouthfuls of cereal.

"Have you looked outside?"

I pushed my chair back and opened the door. A sheet of rain roared down; the downspouts couldn't keep up and the gutters overflowed.

"Jeepers cripes!" I slammed the door. "We're screwed."

Why in the hell did I set traps? I wasn't sure if I said this out loud, but any hope I'd held for sidestepping a rainstorm was gone. The day had just begun and was already a disaster. Still, we had to go. Experience had taught me not to leave a trap line unmonitored. For once, it paid to bring raingear, and I pulled on my pants and coat. We met Dave and drove to the woods where

A wet day of wolf work in northern Idaho.
(Collection of Carter Niemeyer)

we'd hidden our ATVs, which we loaded with our wolf handling gear: catchpole, drug kit and syringe pole.

"I'm guessing we'll be pulling up traps and waiting for a streak of dry weather," I hollered through the downpour.

I pulled my raincoat tight around my face and each of us started our machines down the treacherous dirt road, which by now was shiny mud. The trench between our wheels had become a rushing stream. Rain pelted down and we could hardly see where we were going in the near darkness. Somehow we didn't die. I might not have noticed anyway. I was busy thinking about my traps.

Once we reached the bottom, things were as bad as I'd pictured. The four traps to the east were entirely exposed. I gathered them up and tossed them in the metal crate I'd wired to my ATV. It pissed me off to have to pull traps when I was so close to a wolf pack.

I led the way west toward the other five traps. As we passed through the rendezvous site, we came upon a bull moose walking lazily through the meadow. It was probably the moose that had shed the antlers that the pups were now using for chew toys. Some people think wolves kill everything in sight, but that's not what I've seen. We've hardly scratched the surface when it comes to understanding the complexities of the natural world. Maybe we're not meant to understand it, just to accept it and stop asking questions. This bull moose was literally living among a wolf pack. Only it could tell you why it wasn't afraid.

The first trap to the west of the rendezvous site was still in a set position, but the dirt that covered it had washed away. A wolf could easily avoid this one. I motioned to the guys that we should keep moving. I'd come back for this one later.

As we approached the next one, the area looked all wrong, even in the rain and dim light. The pan cover – the paper that I use to keep dirt from interfering with the trap trigger mechanism – was lying in the road. The trap was gone. The rain, however, had destroyed the drag mark, scuff marks, or anything else that might have told us which way the animal ran.

"Shut off your engines," I waved. "We've got something."

The rain still came down, tapping on us. We were quiet, listening and looking.

"Over there!" Dave pointed.

A wet wolf struggled about 50 yards away, its foot in a trap. The drag had tangled in a bush in the otherwise open meadow.

"You guys get it wrangled while I mix drugs." I was already digging around in my kit, and the men were already in action. In a matter of minutes, they had encircled the wolf and pinned its head to the ground using a catchpole. I pushed a dose of sedative into its hindquarter, and in another 10 minutes, the dripping wolf was out. We each caught our breath. The wolf was a she, and she had somehow ended up with both front paws in the trap. She was on the small side, probably a yearling that had stayed with the pack as a nanny – the pups' caretaker when the adults were away.

I compressed the trap springs and removed the steel from her feet. She seemed uninjured, but she'd probably be sore for a few days. The catch was low across her toe webbings, right where it should be. Catching her higher would have meant a potential injury to bone. The key was to get the animal out of it as soon as possible. The more they struggled, the tighter the trap jaws gripped.

The guys chattered quietly. This was exciting stuff. One of them laid out a blanket on the wet ground and we gingerly moved the wolf onto it. They helped me record measurements on a data sheet, take blood samples, and put an ear tag and radio collar on the wolf. We took turns checking her temperature and monitoring her pulse and respiration. When we'd finished, we covered her with another blanket and left her to recover, which wouldn't take more than another half hour. She would stay warm until we could check on her again. When she was up and moving, her collar would forever betray her identity and location: B-233. She could be located by land or air as long as the battery lasted – a couple of years, maybe as many as five.

There have been a few wolves whose collars lasted ten years or so, but that's unusual. Sometimes wolves chew off the collars, and sometimes the collars just quit functioning, but usually they are reliable. They emit a regular beep on a certain frequency and are generally weatherproof. Considering how a wolf lives, that says a lot about the quality of the electronics contained in a radio collar. There's an old VHF-style (monitored by antennae using line of sight up to about 10 miles) and a newer GPS type (monitored by satellite and subject to computer glitches). What hasn't changed is that a collar's battery only lasts so long, and if it's not replaced before it dies, well, it gets mighty hard to find wolves in the mountains without a signal to go by.

It was light now, and the rain had let up a bit, but we weren't in any danger of drying out. We motored on, ready to pick up the traps and get out of there. But the next one was gone. My jaw dropped. The wolves must have been on the move through this area early the previous night before the rain started. It was all I could figure. We switched off our engines again and scattered, walking carefully, trying to locate our next captive. One of the guys hollered from the forest line.

"We've got a bear!"

Lovely, I muttered. I carried my gear up the hill, but this black bear was a little too feisty to approach with only a six-foot syringe pole. From a distance she looked like a yearling, but once we had her immobilized, I looked at her teeth. She was an old girl, in her declining years at about 150 pounds. Her size may have saved her from being a wall trophy. Too small. I guessed her to be about 15 years old, but with plenty of attitude. She was difficult to sedate because she was thrashing around, so Josh Stanley duct-taped the syringe pole to a skinny, 12-foot tree branch. When he was finished, it looked like a lance. He ran toward the bear in true jousting style and thrust the needle into her as he passed by. It worked. When she conked out, I took the trap off her foot and the four of us carried her to a nearby slope in the trees to sleep it off.

To my utter amazement, the next trap was missing, too. The guys were starting to think this was ridiculous. We set out separately to look, spanning 50 yards in all directions from the trap site.

"Hey, over here," Dave shouted. He had been blithely checking every unlikely crag and hole in the ground, and had come upon a rotten log, four feet in diameter, close to where the trap disappeared. He knelt down, expecting nothing, and was confronted with a very large wolf – the breeding male of the pack, as it turned out. The wolf growled in the dark log, making the wet wood rumble. Dave froze. The wolf stared. I tiptoed to the other end of the log and used a pole to poke the big wolf in the butt with a needle full of sedative.

We repeated the same processing routine and the male wolf became B-234. These wolves, and the others with them, would now be known as the Avery Pack. Thankfully, the last trap was empty, something I never thought I'd be glad about. There were two collars in this pack now. That was enough.

It was still raining and, despite the excitement of the morning, being wet all day had us feeling chilled. We checked on the bear and the female wolf. They had recovered and moved on. It was time for a sandwich before we gathered up the trap I'd left at the beginning of the line. Josh opened his pocketknife and shaved strips of dried pitch from the lodgepole pine we stood under. He put them on the ground with a handful of pine needles and lit the small bundle with a lighter. A campfire in a rainstorm. It felt mighty good.

We had almost finished our sandwiches when we heard something. A wolf. Howling. It couldn't have been more than a hundred yards away. We stopped mid-bite and looked at each other. Another howl. Then another. We whispered and craned our necks. We could see a blondish colored animal trotting back and forth in the dense willows, appearing, then disappearing. The howling was quick and almost frantic. It must be an adult calling its missing pack mates. But after several minutes, I formed a different idea. This howling, and the fact that she seemed annoyed by our presence but unwilling to retreat, meant something. I threw my sandwich crust in the fire.

"I'm gonna pick up that last trap," I said, heading toward the ATV.

"Not without us," Dave said with his mouth full.

We quickly buried the fire and, once again, zoomed off. When we rounded the bend near my set, I braked. What looked like a two-headed wolf was curled up on the ground. Before I could figure out what I was seeing, two wolf pups jumped up from the spot. One scurried across the road. The other stayed behind, its front paw caught in the trap. I shut off my motor and sprinted to it. It couldn't have been caught long. This was what had pissed off the mother wolf. Off in the trees, she howled again.

Freeing pups has to be fast. The more they struggle, the more they can hurt themselves. They're too small to drug, in my opinion, but their teeth can leave an impressive gash if you don't get control of the head quickly. I grabbed the pup by the scruff and pinned its head to the ground. It weighed between 15 and 20 pounds. I freed its foot. There was a dent, but that's all. Dave and Josh snapped photos and looked it over while I held it firm. I released the pup gently, but it sat frozen in fear before creeping away. It broke into a run as it neared a stand of bushy willows. Only then did the hidden adult stop howling.

Later that day, I checked my phone messages.

"Hey Carter, it's Isaac. Hey, your traps over here in the Lochsa caught a 75-pound female at Lost Creek."

I smiled. It had been quite a day.

The Biscuit Basin Wolves

In early 2005, a small pack of wolves silently slipped out of Yellowstone's Madison-Firehole region and navigated ranch and farm country to the west, settling in Idaho. They were known in Yellowstone as the Biscuit Basin wolves, and they were in terrible shape. Researchers in the park believed the pack had fallen on hard times. Most elk and deer leave Yellowstone's high country in the winter, getting out of shoulder-deep snow, and heading for south-facing slopes and lowlands where they can find something to eat. As a result, the wolves have no food except bison, and not many wolf packs can take down those ornery beasts. The Biscuit Basin pack was outcompeted for the elk and deer that lingered just a little too long in the park and had become snowbound. The wolves were skin and bones. So like the elk, they left, looking for food.

One of them didn't last long. Wolf Number 476, a yearling female, wore a collar, and whoever killed her cut it off and threw it in the Falls River, east of Ashton, Idaho. Its battery case and transmitter were waterproof, and even from the depths of the river, it beeped a fast signal, indicating that it had not moved in four hours – a "mortality signal." Sometimes it means the collar fell off, but often it just means dead. Law enforcement agents fished the collar out of the river and publicized a reward for anyone who cared to add to their knowledge about it. No one ever came forward, and no one was arrested.

The next spring, I was working as a seasonal trapper for the Idaho Department of Fish and Game, only a few months after I retired from the federal Fish and Wildlife Service. One of my first assignments for the state was to head east to meet with biologist Lauri Hanauska-Brown. She wanted me to scout for wolves that had been reported near Antelope Flat and Bishop Mountain, close to the Montana border and, as the crow flies, pretty close to Yellowstone. People were seeing them, she said.

I set ten traps just because the area looked like it had potential, but there were no wolves that had traveled the roads. Not even a coyote. We howled. Nothing. So Lauri and I decided instead to spend a day trying to find Yellowstone's missing Biscuit Basin pack, and took along U.S. Forest Service biologist Bryan Aber. The wolves were nearby, somewhere around the Warm River, according to radio collar signals.

There was no way to know whether the wolves had denned that spring. We just assumed they did. It's what a pack will do, if the dynamics are right. We dialed in the collar of the breeding female, wolf Number 340, and drove down the highway, stopping periodically to check our telemetry signal. When we pointed the hand-held antenna out the window toward the north, the signal got stronger. The day was pleasant. We pulled off the road and hiked in.

We only had one real concern: the collared grizzly bear, part of another study in the area, that was last located where we intended to hike. We took two radios, one to monitor each animal. Not all large predators end up wearing research collars,

Idaho Fish and Game biologist Lauri Hanauska-Brown
searches for Biscuit Basin wolf pups.
(Photo by Carter Niemeyer)

just enough of them to try to help wildlife managers figure out things like territories, travel corridors, and breeding success – and to be able to find them if they cause trouble. It's an area of controversy, all this collaring. Tourists in Yellowstone don't like seeing animals wearing collars. Photographers trying to get a shot of a wild wolf really don't like the collars. On one hand, we are eager for the data that collars provide; on the other, we don't need them in order to allow the animals to exist.

At the last minute, I grabbed the bag containing my video camera and we headed into the hills. At a muddy wetland close to the river, we paused. Big mistake. The second we came through the brush, mosquitoes swarmed all over us. We buttoned down and pulled our hats over our ears. I even put on gloves. We had to hurry up and wade across, but nobody was about to ruin field boots. The three of us changed into sandals as fast as we could. We cursed and hopped around, waving and swatting. Mosquitoes blackened us and drilled through our pants. On the opposite bank, we did it in reverse and then kept going. Once we were into the drier meadow, the little bastards left us alone. We chuckled once it was over. Everybody worries about carnivores, but mosquitoes have probably killed more people than any creature on earth.

When a slight breeze drifted in from the south, we decided to keep going north beyond the area where we thought we'd find the pack. We didn't want them picking up our scent. The wolves were probably in a rendezvous site at this time of day. It might make our hike longer, but it could pay off. The wolves seemed to be in the re-growth of an old logging area. The trees were anywhere from six to twenty feet tall, most with branches that swept the ground. We couldn't see very far ahead as we made our approach. The radio signal for the wolf was getting stronger. I figured we were a quarter mile from the pack. We checked the grizzly monitor. No signal. I hoped it stayed that way.

Before making our final approach, we stopped. I moved the handheld antennae slowly back and forth in front of me, turning it gradually, to hone in on the exact location of the wolf.

"You be my eyes," I whispered to Lauri and Bryan. I watched the signal pulse on my receiver like a tiny analog heartbeat. I moved the antennae a little to the right, a little to the left. I turned down the volume and just watched the pulse until it was as strong as it could be.

"There," I whispered, nodding toward pines so dense they seemed like a solid wall. The wolf was only yards in front of us, but we couldn't see it.

"Use hand signals," I added. "Tell me what you see."

We had taken only a few steps when I heard low growling. Bryan was about twenty feet to my left. Lauri was on her haunches next to me, trying to get a look at what was beyond the low branches. We froze. More growling to our right.

I looked at Lauri. She was still hunched down, looking under the trees. Slowly, she raised one finger, then another. Two wolves. I watched the receiver pulse furiously.

More growling and snarling. Then I saw a hairy gray leg. A wolf stood right in front of me in the trees. I wanted to get my video camera, but I didn't dare move. A very slight breeze moved through the trees, almost undetectable.

Two gray wolves stepped into the open not six feet away. One was much larger than the other, but both were adults. Neither wore a radio collar. The smaller of the two rolled on its back, submissively tucking its tail while the other straddled it, baring its teeth.

We froze in our tracks. Then, as fast as this had unfolded, it was over. One of the wolves let out a startled bark and then both vanished into the pines, leaving but a few branches waving behind them. We looked at each other and smiled. It was a million-dollar moment.

I motioned that I was still getting a strong radio signal straight ahead. The collared female was close by, right in front of us. We inched forward at a little faster pace in case other wolves might be slipping away with the pups.

We came to an opening in the trees where a logging crew had left a huge slash pile. It had to be thirty or forty feet wide and nearly twenty feet high, all big lodgepole timbers lying in a woven tangle. I caught Lauri and Bryan's eyes and pointed to the pile. I was willing to bet the female was inside.

There were two big openings in the pile and tufts of wolf fur clung to the logs where they'd come and gone. I looked in one hole, then slipped my video camera out of its case and set the case on the ground, along with the radio receiver and antennae. I motioned to my partners to walk around the back side of the pile and watch that opening while I kept an eye on the one in front of me.

Lauri and Bryan disappeared behind the slash pile. Everything was quiet. I picked up my camera, planning to switch it on. As I stood there, an enormous white wolf burst out of the opening in front of me, trampled my camera bag, sending it tumbling, and then disappeared into the pines.

I got a look at it in the two seconds before it was gone. It was wearing a radio collar. If it had wanted to kill me, I wouldn't have had time to react. It looked to be in good condition – better than the scrawny critter that left Yellowstone.

But what it wanted was to escape. I scampered for my telemetry equipment. It was the female, Number 340.

Wolves are timid. Curious, but timid. They don't go crazy defending their young the way bears do. Maybe they figure they can always make more puppies. Their first order of business is self-preservation. Most people don't buy that, but they've watched too many movies about killer wolves. Once, many years after the Biscuit Basin pack incident, I worked with the Spokane Tribe of Indians to collar a wolf on their reservation in Washington. The biologist, Katie Eaton, and I sneaked in on a pack and found ourselves surrounded by barking, howling wolves. I whispered to her. "Are you scared?" She was pregnant and might have had good reason to be concerned. But she just looked at me with a huge smile. It was the coolest thing she'd ever experienced. And both of us lived through it.

Number 340's radio signal slowly faded as Lauri and Bryan re-emerged from the other side of the slash pile. I whispered about what I'd just seen. I decided to make whimpering sounds like a wolf pup to see if I could get the pack to react. They did, snarling and grumbling from their fortress of fluffy trees.

Bryan and I walked around and examined the well-worn wolf trails, the wolf fuzz stuck on the log pile, and the contents of pup scat that lay all over the place. It was obvious they'd found a better home here. They were eating, anyway. Lauri decided to climb up on the slash pile and get a look inside. She wormed her way into the hole. Only her boots stuck out. Before long she put her arm out and started reporting with her fingers. One. Two.... Bryan walked to the far end of the slash pile. A wolf pup nosed its way out briefly, then retreated. I climbed up on the pile and started poking sticks through it, trying to move pups around. After a while, Lauri climbed down. She'd had three pups within a foot of her face. One even snarled at her.

On the hike back to the truck, we recounted the day, feeling thankful not to have run into a crabby grizzly, and wondering about the pack and the pups and whether anyone knew they were there. We talked about the future of wolves and whether they could ever be tolerated like any other predator, and whether the Biscuit Basin pack could stay out of trouble. I tried to sound hopeful. This area held great abundance for the wolves, but it wasn't Yellowstone. The dangers in Idaho were many. A hard winter could hit this area as easily as Yellowstone. I was certain poachers were around, evidenced by the wolf collar that had been thrown in the river. Then there was the matter of the

Biscuit Basin wolves fending off other packs that might want that territory, which is always likely for newcomers.

We talked as we waded through seas of white mule's ears that covered the sunny meadows like giant daisies. At the Warm River, we once again changed into our sandals while mosquitoes once again tried their level best to eat us. But this time, we hardly noticed.

Black Phantoms

I grabbed the elk, or what was left of it, by one hind leg and dragged it across the two-lane highway, over broken glass and skid marks. Down a small hill and across a hundred yards of sagebrush we went, past where seven of my wolf traps lay waiting in the cool dirt. A light rain began to fall. In a few hours, it would be dark.

It was early June 2007 when Idaho Department of Fish and Game officers reported wolves – all of them black – eating on the elk carcass along the edge of the highway near Ketchum in an area called Phantom Hill. People kept calling. Observant drivers slowed and stopped on the shoulder of Highway 75. Others sped by without noticing a wolf was standing just feet away. The wolves were fast becoming famous around the Sun Valley area, something that seemed to irritate wolf managers back in Boise.

The state was now in charge, and had been since the feds handed over the reins in January 2006. If left to themselves, Idaho Fish and Game biologists would have been mostly tolerant of wolves, but they were under strict orders from the governor's office via the Fish and Game Commission to "manage" wolves with an iron fist, mostly because the feds had dared to bring them back. In the first years after reintroduction, the Nez Perce Tribe had monitored wolf populations in Idaho – something the state was supposed to do, but the Legislature forbade. Softhearted state biologists kept their opinions to themselves for fear of inadvertently shortening their careers. Nurturing the sour taste left after reintroduction, Idaho politicians grumbled loudly about what wolves might do to elk and deer populations as well as ranchers' cows and sheep munching away on federal land – a good 60 percent of the state. State lawmakers wanted wolves gone, but Idaho, like Montana and Wyoming, is stuck with federal Endangered Species Act rules to ensure that the near extinction of this animal will never happen again. Trying to balance it all, state biologists were undoubtedly sick of the whole thing, and they were only getting started. Now their phones were ringing about the Phantom Hill wolves.

I was on the state's payroll as a seasonal trapper as I had been the year before. Being able to catch wolves was important enough to the new wolf managers that they were willing to overlook my status as a retired fed, heavily involved in reintroduction, and an outspoken advocate of all wildlife, but especially wolves. Wolves had become my specialty, and I believed I had gotten them in pretty good shape in Idaho before management changed hands and I retired. I drove mountain back roads looking for signs of packs whose collars had quit functioning, narrowing down the wolves' locales and setting traps to catch them. Sometimes I accompanied new biologists who hadn't ever trapped a wolf, and taught them how. Other days, I ventured out to talk to people who were having trouble with wolves bothering their livestock. For every person who hated wolves, I found four or five who didn't.

As for the Phantom Hill wolves, I hoped to keep them away from the dangers of the highway – and closer to my trap line – by moving the elk carcass. All day, the wolves had visited the carcass, taking away softball-sized chunks until there was little left but bones and hide. The wolves were just being opportunistic. They hadn't killed the elk. It was a car casualty. Cars do at least as much killing as wolves ever will.

Once the work of the day was finished, I sat in my truck on the highway shoulder, about a hundred yards from where the elk carcass had been, and wrote in my field journal. I noted everything that happened, as I have done every day of my career since 1973. The Phantom Hill wolves were spending a lot of time next to the highway. No wonder everybody had seen them. I wrote a brief account of the fifteen or twenty cyclists who had passed me an hour or so earlier. The ones in the lead never looked up from the pavement, but one guy in the middle shouted and pointed, "There's a wolf!" Then the ones in the back nearly piled up trying to get a look. The cyclists spooked one younger animal and it slinked up the valley. The old gray-faced male, one I'd looked at good and long through binoculars yesterday, tore off another piece of elk and followed. I also jotted a few notes about a guy who pulled up next to me and rolled down his window.

"Man, this is cool!" he said about the wolves up ahead. "This is the second wolf I've ever seen." I wasn't too surprised to learn the fellow's last name was Wolf.

These side stories were incidental to the facts of the day. I wrote in detail about who I met, what we talked about, how many traps I'd set, where they were. Everything. In the back of my journal were three or four pages filled with names and phone numbers, gate codes to U.S. Forest Service roads, all kinds of stuff. The hard cover spine was fraying and the journal's pages were nearly all filled. I'd need a new one soon, I murmured to myself.

I closed the book and tucked it away. I needed to go see if my tent had blown over during a wind that had moved through earlier. Then three dark dots appeared in the valley about a half-mile in front of me. Three Phantom Hill wolves were walking toward my traps. One was the lanky wolf that was scared of the cyclists. Its fur was not completely black, but slightly salt and pepper in parts. The group sniffed the air, then approached the elk carcass I'd dragged there. I thought I might have a wolf snapped at any second.

Suddenly truck headlights appeared behind me and a man got out and slammed his door. I watched him in my rearview mirror. He crunched his way up to me in the gravel. I didn't want him seeing what I was seeing in case he was one of those idiots who shoot from the road at whatever is moving out there. I'd already started my engine.

"Did you know there are wolves around here? People have been seeing wolves right along this highway," he announced louder than he needed to.

"Yeah, I've heard that, too," I said, and wished him a good evening as I drove off.

"There's three black wolves that come down that ridge to the left of that small pine tree," Lee Garwood pointed at the hills. Lee was an Idaho conservation officer. "They come right through that little draw past those willows and work their way across that opening."

Roger Olson was with him. He was recently retired as Lee's boss. The two were fit and trim and didn't take shit from anybody. Theirs were the types of eyes I could use more often when I'm looking for wolves. Lawmen pay attention to the details that most others miss. In the days before I moved the elk carcass from the highway, they'd been out here sizing up the Phantom Hill pack for me.

Lee had to get back to other duties, but Roger offered to stay. He knew enough about trapping to know I'd want to be where the wolves were going, not where they've been, and he had helped me figure out where, in the sea of sagebrush, I ought to place my traps.

Depending on what kind of hunting success they're having, it sometimes takes a couple weeks or more for wolves to make a big loop, circling back to haunts they visited earlier, just to see what's up. If I trapped too close to the elk carcass, I was going to hook a bear. Already, several big ones had discovered it.

People were getting more problematic, too. The local newspaper published a story about the wolves, complete with color photos. Hikers started appearing near my trap line. I wondered about all of this, especially how people seemed to be at least fifty percent of any problem a wolf encounters. I decided to pull my traps and try again later. At this rate, I'd have a bear, a dog, or a hiker caught in one. Things needed to settle down. With the deliciousness of the rotten carcass, the wolves had little reason to be enticed by the stinky lure I'd applied to my trap line. And there was one more thing: Lava Lake Land and Livestock was getting ready to turn loose a band of sheep – about 1,500 – right in the middle of the Phantom Hill area.

We waved them off, and to Lava Lake's credit, its manager decided to put the sheep somewhere else. Lava Lake's status as predator friendly was important to its operation, so its owners cooperated with wolf managers. They didn't want dead sheep – or dead wolves. Other sheep owners weren't so responsive. Federal grazing allotments can't be swapped that easily, and it's even harder to convince ranchers that they should save wolves by moving their livestock. When bears and lions eat their animals, ranchers have for generations simply contacted the federal government, and within a day or so, the predators are killed. Once wolves became protected by the Endangered Species Act, many people breathed a sigh of relief that at least the animals could never again be completely exterminated – legally, anyway.

Before I left the area, a friend, Cindi Hillemeyer, offered to help. She knew about wolves and hiking and everything else about the ridges and valleys where the Phantom Hill wolves lived. She climbed the aspen-covered hills and howled, hoping to entice the pack to come out in the open so she could see exactly how many we were dealing with. To her utter surprise, she was successful, counting three pups among the adults. She snapped a few photos and sneaked out again.

I knew I had to come back.

On June 26, I returned to Phantom Hill. This time I brought my wife, Jenny, with me and set five traps back in the same area. Since my last visit a couple of weeks earlier, cars had hit three more elk on Highway 75. Roger Olson took it upon himself to drag their carcasses off the highway and dump them halfway up the valley toward the aspen grove where Cindi had seen the pups.

I kept my traps away from the rotting carcasses, trying to avoid bears. The whole area smelled pretty bad. I wasn't real sure about this. It seemed like there were still too many olfactory distractions to get any of the pack interested in my sets.

Within a day, tracks showed the bears had sprung two of my five traps, but didn't get caught. I could see where wolves had been coming and going when Roger, Jenny and I surveyed the area each morning. The wolves had regularly trampled the grass through an hourglass-shaped patch of brush. One left a fresh track in the soft dirt pushed up by a pocket gopher. This was the perfect place for a blind set – one with no scent – placed where a wolf might step in the course of traveling. The wolves were already using the narrow path. It was perfect. I put in a trap.

At first light the next morning, the three of us converged at the highway pull off and looked through binoculars to see if there was any action before we walked into it. Two black wolves sat on the slope above the elk carcasses. They kept getting up and pacing, then howling. They were upset. I was willing to bet we'd caught one of their buddies.

We divvied up my wolf capture gear and walked single file through the sagebrush. First trap: nothing. Second trap: nothing. We checked four traps. No wolves. But the two wolves on the slope above us still howled. There was still one more trap to check, the one on the gopher mound.

Twenty yards shy of the trap, we could see small willows shaking. A couple of twigs snapped. Then I heard one of my favorite sounds – the rattle of a trap chain.

"Wait here," I whispered. Roger and Jenny stopped. I hoped we didn't have a pissed-off bear. They're never happy about having their toes pinched.

I went ahead, catching a flash of black as I moved around the brush, slowly. Ahead of me, a young wolf stared back. I wanted to see how it was caught and if there was any chance it could pull out. It was a good catch, the left front foot held in the trap by several toes. I retreated to my partners, just as slowly, and measured a syringe of Telazol. Roger distracted the wolf while I pushed the drug into its hip. While we waited for it to work, I wondered if this was the cautious one that had retreated from the bicyclists. Roger looked at his watch. Eight minutes had passed. The wolf was limp, but aware. Its eyes remained open. We went to work as the sun was cresting the ridge above us.

It's always better to have a couple of people helping with a capture. So often I've been alone, with no one to share the excitement – or to help weigh a wolf on my spring scale, take its temperature, or take care of any of the dozen things that need doing in the thirty minutes or so the wolf is immobile. Some wake up faster. It depends on their metabolism and the drug dosage. Being alone on a trap line also means there's no one to take photos of the whole process. This time, Jenny clicked away on the digital camera I'd received from my office mates as a retirement gift.

I compressed the trap springs and freed the wolf's foot. No swelling. Good. A perfect catch, in my judgment. A compression injury is the thing I worry about the most. This one's foot would be sore for a day or two, but nothing serious. Wolves have some of the toughest feet around, but traps can be unforgiving if you don't know what you're doing. If you plan to release a trapped animal back into the wild, its feet need to be in good condition. Wolves hunt with their feet as much as their fangs. They have to be able to cover great distances to follow their food, or their lives are over.

I lifted one hind leg to see that this was an un-bred female, and opened her mouth to check for obstructions like twigs. This wolf wasn't particularly a fighter, and unlike so many others, she didn't go crazy trying to escape when I first approached her. She had nothing in her mouth. She didn't even bite at the trap. Her incisors were white and sharply cusped. She was probably a yearling. Jenny covered the wolf's face with a bandana to protect her eyes.

Roger and I made a sling and he helped me weigh her on my spring scale. Eighty pounds exactly. Jenny wrote on the data sheet while I dictated numbers, took a DNA sample and measured the young wolf. Roger helped me move her around and took her temperature, pulse and respiration. Before I put the collar on her, I dialed in its frequency on my radio receiver. It was exactly where the manufacturer had set it: 218.994. Sometimes collars arrive with frequencies that are off a number or two. I wrote the number inside her collar with a Sharpie. When the collar was the right fit, I used a special wrench to tighten the brass screws. Then I took pliers from my kit and punched blue plastic Idaho Department of Fish and Game ear tags in each ear. From now on, this wolf was known as B-326.

Judith, one of the Phantom Hill wolves, near Ketchum, Idaho.
(Photo by Jenny Niemeyer)

"I hate those," Jenny said. "Why do they have to be ear-tagged?" Blood ran down the wolf's soft, black ears.

"In case the collar falls off or stops working," I said. I wasn't a fan, either, but this was protocol and I was just an employee. The wolves had started looking more and more like Christmas trees after we were done with them, especially when we were instructed to wrap radio collars with neon orange tape. Wildlife Services wanted the tape so when they flew in to gun down a problem pack they could tell which ones were collared. They'd sometimes not been able to tell, and killed collared wolves. Once that happened, the rest of the pack's whereabouts became unknown.

It was too pretty out to think about that stuff. The air was cool and clear and the sun was just coming over the ridge when we finished. Everything looked fresh and innocent, and instead of the stench of rotting elk, the pungent scent of trampled sage-brush hung in the air.

B-326 was beginning to stir.

"I think we should call this one Judith," Jenny said. She'd been squatting down awhile over the drugged wolf, dribbling water from a plastic bottle into its mouth. It licked absently.

"Steve ain't gonna like that," I said.

Steve Nadeau was the wolf supervisor for this region of the state. He didn't like the idea of naming wolves. I had to agree. People got worked up enough already. Naming them just made everything more personal when the wolves got in trouble. It's the least scientific thing you can do with a wild animal, but I suppose it's what you do when you have a heart.

"She's a female version of a Judas wolf." Jenny continued, giving this bony, black wolf a drink until her bottle was empty. She was talking about the betrayal factor. The Judas wolf is the pack member wearing a collar – betraying the whereabouts of its family. It was a term wolf managers had used for a long time.

She touched the wolf's head, then gathered the camera and her backpack and walked away.

And that was that.

Judith recovered from her traumatic morning and wandered uphill through the shadows and sunlight, appearing now and again in the tall grass and sagebrush. She stopped occasionally, looking at us, then continued on until at last she was out of sight.

Not a month later, the Phantom Hill wolves began killing sheep across the highway, and the state decided it needed another collar in the pack to make sure the wolves could be tracked if something happened to Judith. The feds would handle this one.

Soon after that, I had a few days off and headed to a wolfers' rendezvous in the woods near Ketchum. We had started trying to get together each summer, all of us who had been involved in wolf research and capture over the years. Wolfers used to be the guys who killed wolves for bounty. We'd adopted the term and turned it on its head, recasting it as the people who capture wolves and let them go again, wearing radio or satellite collars. Our group had differing opinions on wolves, but our work brought us together. We had become far flung, and a campout together was a rarity. It was also a good chance for gossip.

"Hey, did you hear?" asked a low voice in the flickering darkness. Another trapper I'd known for years was talking about collaring the latest Phantom Hill wolf.

"One of our guys beat the shit out of it with a chunk of lodgepole while it was still drugged." He went on to say that the wolf didn't move for days, according to the radio collar. The wood-wielding trapper thought maybe he'd killed it, so he went back to check.

"I guess it lived because the signal started moving away," the trapper said, tossing a stick into the fire. "Must've heard the asshole on his trail again."

Silence. We drank our beers. What do you say to something this horrendous? Our group of about five was away from others, who were yucking it up and roasting marshmallows. This didn't sound like a tall tale to me. In fact, I wondered who else had done similar things. It wasn't enough to hate wolves for being back; some people needed to torture them. Too often, federal trappers believe they work for the ranchers. It was a chronic condition of the outfit, and one I'd struggled in vain to change for much of the 26 years I worked there. Things are still no different, with some Wildlife Services trappers letting wolves die slowly in traps, gassing puppies out of dens, and keeping a running tally of the dead by marking their yellow airplane with paw print decals, the way an ace fighter would. They believed heartily in the old adage: The only good wolf is a dead wolf.

If the Phantom Hill wolves kept it up, the State of Idaho was ready to drop the axe, no matter how popular the animals had become. They'd killed more than a dozen of John Faulkner's sheep across the highway from where I trapped Judith, and kept coming back for more. That the sheep were driven across Idaho on foot right into known wolf territory was not considered part of the problem.

Suzanne Stone of Defenders Of Wildlife wanted to try something new in the Phantom Hill area: a long-term project of hazing wolves out of the places where sheep graze (and get killed by wolves) every year. Why not? Killing wolves never prevents the problem from rearing up again, I urged Faulkner. You just end up with more wolves again next year. The sheep man wasn't thrilled, but went along with it. It was Blaine County, a rare bastion of environmentalism in the state, so it made sense to do the project there. I helped the volunteers map the area and showed them how to use cracker shells, fladry and other means of scaring away wolves. One of the best non-lethal ways of dealing with these carnivores is for people simply to be present among the sheep. People will make wolves go the other way almost every time.

The project went on for several years, and Faulkner grumbled about it, but mostly went along. But each time the wolves went after Faulkner's sheep, the agencies dropped out of the project and started killing wolves, until there were no wolves left in the area and virtually nothing for project volunteers to do. Even the local county commissioner was unsuccessful in keeping wolves alive. Projects like this are voluntary for ranchers. Killing wolves for killing livestock has always been their preferred way of doing business. The only way to discover whether non-lethal methods of protecting livestock are successful is if the wolves are afforded a chance to live through the experiment.

State wildlife officials weren't interested in helping Suzanne with non-lethal deterrence. They couldn't stop her, but their only interest was in reducing the number of wolves down to the bare minimum needed to keep the feds off their backs. Special attention given to certain wolves just made the phone ring more when they decided to gun them down. In their eyes, all wolves would eventually cause trouble, and they didn't appreciate Suzanne pointing out the shortcomings of their management style, even though a percentage of the federal money Idaho receives to manage wolves is supposed to be spent on non-lethal means of dealing with the animal.

State game managers weren't above using the Phantom Hill wolves for entertainment, however. Just before real trouble began with Faulkner's sheep, they asked me to be at a regional mountain lion workshop in Sun Valley and guide a short wolf-watching expedition for state biologists as a distraction to all of the talk about lions. I arrived a day early to scout the Phantom

Hill pack. Good thing the state didn't execute them last year, I thought as I pointed my telemetry antennae toward the hill, waiting to hear Judith's collar.

Wolf watching is something the agency opposes for the general public, even though most of it would happen on federal lands in remote places. If everybody who got a look at them – or tried to – had to pay for the experience, the state would be flush.

In Idaho, as in most other states, hunters and anglers keep wildlife agencies running by purchasing licenses and tags. Some folks have suggested broadening the interest base – and increasing funding – by adding a non-consumptive "wildlife watching" tag, but state officials everywhere have been bullied into inaction because sportsmen don't want non-hunters to have a say. No state has yet created such a thing. The closest conservationists can get to buying a seat at the table is purchasing a non-game license plate, but even then the money is sometimes used to kill wildlife, and not just in Idaho. Many wildlife commissioners insinuate that a license plate is somewhat sissified; it doesn't carry the seriousness of a hunting or fishing license. Maybe state officials are afraid they'll be outvoted and outspent by environmentalists. It would explain why, in 2012, Idaho lawmakers felt the need to amend the state constitution with a clause that guarantees hunting, fishing and trapping – forever.

It wasn't long before I found Judith and B-333, the collared, breeding male of the pack, and probably Judith's father. They were hanging around the Sawtooth National Recreation Area, just out of Ketchum as the crow flies. The next day, snow swirled around our small crowd. The ground was white. Spring comes late and winter early to this part of the world. My scouting didn't pay off for the tour. We saw no wolves. But in the pale light of the next morning, several biologists from Utah made the trek again and spotted four black wolves on a hill. It was the entire pack. Soon I learned that six puppies had been born, bringing the Phantom Hill pack to ten.

On the heels of the Sun Valley field trip, a crew from ABC's Nightline flew in. They wanted to get the famous wolves on film. The Phantom Hill pack's proximity to star-studded Ketchum probably made them the most talked-about wolves in the country at the time.

The crew loaded outrageously expensive camera gear into my truck bed and climbed into the back with it. They wanted to talk to local sheep ranchers, too, and asked me to set it up. I drove slowly down the highway toward Phantom Hill, pulled out my antennae and dialed in Judith. The film crew busied themselves putting together a tri-pod and lens. A car containing the show's reporter and producer followed me.

"Stop! Stop! I see her!" The photographer yelled from the back of my truck. I pulled over as smoothly as possible. We sat silent and motionless and the camera barely made a sound as it rolled. Later, he showed me what he'd captured: Judith hunting down a ground squirrel and eating it.

After hearing different versions of how many wolves were in this pack, I decided to walk into the Phantom Hill rendezvous site myself. I hiked into the area from the Boulder Creek side of the ridge and walked to the top. There I had a good vantage point above the aspen grove where the wolves had lived the year before.

I sat down in front of a huge boulder, my silhouette broken by the sagebrush in front of me. I howled. I was hoping for a pack response, but got just a single pup. It kept howling, then appeared out of the aspens, looking around frantically as if it were lost. I howled again, hoping more of the pack would appear. Instead the black pup came racing toward me. Damn!

Then my cell phone rang.

I didn't know I could even get a phone call up here. I fumbled with it, trying to make it shut up the only way I knew how: answer it.

"Where are you? Whattaya doin'?" It was Rick Williamson. This is the way we start almost every phone call with each other.

Rick was the federal Wildlife Services trapper in Arco, Idaho, and a good friend. Unlike many others in his line of business, he was a reasonable, professional fellow, and prankster as well. He and I were well versed in livestock investigations, and the angst between ranchers and wolf lovers. He was an expert at gadgetry that made some of the non-lethal wolf deterrents work.

"I'm at Phantom Hill," I whispered. "I have a black wolf pup running up to me so I gotta call you back."

Rick laughed.

"Where are you, anyway?" He wouldn't give up.

"I gotta go!" I whispered, and hung up on him.

The wolf pup had traveled about 100 yards and was standing in the sagebrush, still howling and looking for what it must have thought was a parent. I didn't move or attempt to lure the pup closer. I didn't want it approaching me. Wolves need to stay away from people for their own good. I could have fired a gun into the air, but I didn't have one. I have never carried a gun when doing wolf fieldwork. Only bear work made me that nervous.

After five minutes of running from side to side, howling and searching, the pup tucked its tail and slunk back to the aspens. When it disappeared, I crept away. The pack must have been moving the pups and had yet to return for this one.

At my truck, I called Rick and explained myself. He had sounded sort of irritated when we hung up.

"I kinda believed you after I thought about it for awhile," he chuckled.

While people made the Phantom Hill wolves famous, people and their ever-growing creep into the wild countryside were the common denominator whenever something went south. The wolves followed elk into Ketchum's backyards and killed them, scaring residents into believing that they and their dogs were next. People were terrified by the amount of blood and the drag marks, but that didn't stop the residents of an upscale development who lured 150 elk to artificial feeding grounds — and then worried the wolves would discover the tame animals. One young member of the pack jumped a fence to check out a couple of malamutes, and quickly jumped out again. After a few of these incidents, state biologists used a helicopter to chase the Phantom Hill wolves out of Ketchum proper. Then the wolves killed a mountain lion in the foothills nearby, sneaking in on it as it scavenged an elk carcass. The wolves were fun to observe at a distance, but scary up close.

Judith's collar lasted several years before the battery went dead. She and a look-alike sister traveled together. The two seemed to be good at avoiding people, becoming just silhouettes on a ridge before disappearing from view. In 2008, wolves were assigned game status in Idaho, which meant they could be hunted, and later, trapped and snared. Once out from under the thumb of the feds, the state's main goal became to knock the hell out of wolves, down to the population level agreed upon years earlier: 15 breeding pair or 150 wolves. The state charged what it felt was a reasonable sum: $11.50 per tag.

Everyone knew that eventually wolves would come off the endangered list and be hunted. For some people, it didn't happen soon enough, while others believed wolves should never be delisted. Wolves remain a special case — a species that probably needs a special set of federal rules to protect them forever. The fact that wolves offend some folks so easily is evidence that we're not as tough as we used to be. We want the landscape scrubbed of everything that scares us or is inconvenient. In that sense, the wolves have won, I suppose, because no matter what we've thrown at them since reintroduction, they are back every year, causing an uproar. I just hoped that some of the un-collared, cleverer Phantom Hill wolves had slipped away.

In 2009, cars killed a couple of Phantom Hill wolves, including the old male who survived the beating. The breeding female of the pack disappeared shortly after the death of her mate. When a pack loses the dominant female, it often dissolves. Wildlife Services shot another member of the pack for killing sheep, despite the Defenders of Wildlife project that aimed to keep the peace. By 2011, state biologists drew a line through the pack's name. Like so many packs in Idaho – Thorn Creek, Archie, Timberline – the wolves had offended too many people and killed one too many sheep or calves. They were a fearsome pain in the ass, not meant for today's lifestyle.

By 2013, when Idaho's nearly year-round wolf season began, the Phantom Hill pack was merely a legend. Remember them? All black. Pretty rare. Then a hunter brought a wolf into a check station near Ketchum. He also had shot her puppy as it stood nearby, throwing both of them in the back of his pickup. It was all perfectly legal. The mother wolf was black – sort of salt and pepper. She looked more than a few years old. Her muzzle was graying and she wore a radio collar that was old and scuffed and dented. Its battery was dead. The check station biologist bent over the dead wolf, unscrewed the collar and turned it over.

It read: 218.994. Judith.

The Hunters

August 2010 had been a sleepy, hot month, but now the first of many kinds of elk hunts was underway and a group of archery hunters had set up camp along the road. I waved at them by lifting my index finger off the steering wheel. That's how many drivers who pass each other on narrow dusty roads acknowledge folks. Campers in Idaho's backcountry wave a lot, so I lifted my finger a lot. The guys had picked a nice location. Bear Valley Creek sparkled beside them. Big mountains stood as the backdrop. But a guy in camo was frantically waving me down.

I slid my telemetry receiver under the seat and pulled up next to him. I'd been using the receiver to locate collared wolves. Hiding it was almost a habit. I didn't know what kind of person I was about to meet, and I didn't want him knowing what I was doing before I could size him up. Some hunters weren't too happy about having wolves around. It was bad enough driving a truck with Idaho Department of Fish and Game emblazoned on both doors.

"You a game warden?" The big fellow hooked his arms over my window almost before I'd finished rolling it down.

"No, sir," I said. "You need one?"

"So what are you doing if you're not up here arresting people?" He was trying to be funny, I thought.

I wondered if maybe he needed arresting.

I turned off my engine as a way to stall for a moment. I was measuring the amount of information this guy really required. Who knows, maybe they've seen something that could help me.

"I'm looking for wolves."

I waited for it.

"Wolves, huh? He's looking for wolves," he called to his buddies. Four of them were now almost to my truck door.

You either liked them or hated them, but wolves rarely failed to generate conversation, especially at a hunting camp.

"Yep. There's usually a pack around here this time of year," I said.

The men had been camped out for a couple of days, but when I asked if they'd heard wolves howling at night, they looked at each other. Nope.

"So what are you going to do when you find the wolves?" the first hunter asked, heading toward smartass.

"I'm gonna catch it and stick a radio collar on it," I said.

The men looked at each other. A couple of them raised their eyebrows.

"And how are you going to do that?"

It used to be that I didn't want people I met along a road to know what I was doing, poking around the backcountry, examining the dust for tracks, sticking an antennae out the window. But over the years, I'd had a change of heart. I was never one to creep quietly away from controversy, so why should I do it with wolves? Now I expected it, and when the topic finally came up (it always did), I was ready.

A black wolf, now collared, slinks away from me in Bear Valley.
(Photo by Carter Niemeyer)

I stepped out of my truck and the men followed me to the back. I opened the tailgate and slid a sealed plastic tub to the edge. I'd spent a lot of time cleaning and storing my traps, but figured spoiling one here might be worth it. I pulled on a pair of gloves and opened the tub. I lifted a wolf trap from its dark nest of juniper branches, a scent-masking trick I'd picked up years ago. I unwound the trap's eight-foot chain and strung the whole thing out on the tailgate. The guys stepped forward.

"That's a hell of trap," one said. "OK if we touch it?" His hand was already moving toward it. They handed it back and forth, examining it from every angle, feeling its weight.

"So do these traps hurt 'em or break their legs?"

This had become my favorite question. I took the trap and put it on ground, compressed the springs and set it. I stood, holding the waiting jaws. Then I thrust my hand in.

They jumped back. I was clearly crazy. The jaws snapped so fast it took a second for the men to register what had happened.

"What the fu–?" one started.

I tried to keep a straight face.

"It don't hurt 'em too bad." I gestured while I talked. The trap chain rattled. "Their foot might be sore for awhile. That's all."

Silence.

"Doesn't that hurt?" one asked.

"Well, maybe a little." I bent down and again compressed the springs with my feet and the trap jaws fell open. "It ain't comfy, but you can see it didn't break my hand."

"So, if you catch a wolf, what does the radio collar look like?" We were on to part two.

I pulled out a Telonics brand VHF radio collar from my backpack and showed everyone the stiff, inch-and-a-half wide, heavy duty collar. It weighed about a pound and was dark brown with sewn edges. A sealed transmitter bulged on one side, which emitted a specific radio frequency. I showed them how I would adjust the double-punched holes to fit a wolf's neck, which ranged up to about 22 inches, and bolt it in place with a special wrench. They passed the collar around. I pulled the receiver from its hiding place under the front seat. I showed them how I would track a wolf wearing one of these collars and which antennae I would use depended on the situation.

One question led to another and another. I showed them how I would immobilize a wolf with a syringe pole, or "jab stick." We stood at my tailgate and talked for an hour, the conversation wandering here and there. Everybody was in a pretty good mood, although I'm not sure they planned it that way at the start. They were polite compared to a lot of hunters I'd run across. They wanted to know how I learned all of this, and what made me think I could catch a wolf that easily? It's what I do, I said. I was a trapper. I'd spent a lot of years learning how to make a predator come and step in an area about six-inches square. The secret has always been knowing where they are, and I was in the process of trying to narrow it down when I ran into these guys.

"I know they're around. I just gotta find them." I said.

Yeah, sure.

"Well, thanks," the main hunter said. We all shook hands, and they headed back to their trailers. It was getting dark and I wanted to find a high, open spot to howl. I had a fleeting thought that I probably should have taken the men with me. They'd never heard wolves howl. But I didn't know too much about these guys, even after talking with them awhile. I didn't want to put the wolves in danger.

I drove slowly, headlights off, and stopped at the main Dagger Falls road. At the far end of it was where reintroduction happened many years ago and where the wolves had done fine, despite us. There was not a breath of wind. A star appeared overhead. This was my favorite time of year.

I stepped out onto the gravel as quietly as I could manage and stood for a minute, inhaling the evening freshness, deciding where I might be if I were a wolf. The quiet invaded my ears. Then I cupped my hands around my mouth and let go a series of long, pleading howls. I listened. I memorized the dark fingers of timber in the distance. Remembering such land features was helpful if I could get the wolves to respond, and as I was about to howl again, I heard it, echoing and bouncing its way across the valley, a chorus of ghostly, far-off cries. First, the deep one of an adult, then another, then several higher voices – wolf pups. Heard together they were like a chord struck on an organ in a great hall. Here I was, all alone, experiencing one of the great sounds of nature. It seemed like most of the time I had no one to share this with. Most people were too busy scurrying around to go camp out for a week. I couldn't offer gourmet food or other frivolities, but I could offer this.

We talked, me and the wolves, probably for half an hour. Only shadows and deep blue silence stood between us. I don't know what we talked about, but I spurred them on when they probably wanted to get on with their nightly hunt. Eventually they went quiet, and I gave up. Surely the hunters heard all of that; I wasn't that far from their camp. When I passed by, however, their trailer windows glowed in pleasant oblivion.

Conditions for trapping the next morning were perfect: dry and cool. But it was going to be more work than usual. I put my gear in a backpack and hooked several traps over each other and carried them, three in each gloved hand. For whatever good it would do, I was trying to keep my scent off of them. This particular part of Bear Valley was within The Frank – federal wilderness. No vehicles allowed. Theoretically no piece of machinery is allowed, at least nothing motorized. It seems like that would include things like animal traps. But wilderness and designations like it are somewhat arbitrary. The rules can be bent until they snap, depending on who you are and what you're doing there. I couldn't drive to the area I'd chosen, but I could invade the place with traps.

There were no trails to work with, and that made things more difficult, too. On this morning, I put traps where I thought the wolves might emerge from the trees. Wolves don't often wander aimlessly all over the place. They prefer trails and roads. Our obsession with crisscrossing the forests with roads has made it easier for many species to travel, but it also puts them at risk of being seen more easily, and therefore, killed more easily. But in Bear Valley, there were no roads, or at least, very few.

I finished digging in traps before the sun crested the ridge, and I left. I tried not to touch much, but I was probably leaving my scent everywhere, and for all I knew, the wolves were watching my every move. We don't know what sees us. I'm certain, however, that I am watched by creatures that are much more adept at survival than I am. On the short drive back to the Bear Valley cabin where I was staying, I was surprised to see the group of hunters standing around camp. Shouldn't they be on a mountaintop chasing elk? They waved me in.

"So did you find your wolves?" The main hunter leaned on my window again.

I smiled. "You must have heard them howling last night."

They looked at each other.

"Where were they howling?"

"Right over there," I pointed toward the wide-open, golden meadow. "About a mile from your pillow."

He turned to his buddies, but they shook their heads. They quizzed me about how many, and if they seemed to be getting closer to their camp. I suggested they camp up high, away from water and noise, if they wanted to hear wolves, but they didn't seem too eager.

I had no wolf in my traps when I walked in to check them the next day. Being so close to wolves and not catching one sends up red flags in my mind. Could the wolves have left the country? It wouldn't be the first time. But then as I headed back, I noticed a very fresh wolf track in a gopher mound within 50 yards of my truck. The tracks were coming from the main road and going west. I set down my pack and picked my way along slowly, following the prints. One here, one there. Gopher mounds are a great help in tracking animals when roads and trails get packed down. The wolf had cut away from the road and followed a sandy, dry wash. The fine sand gave up the wolf's corridor, and where he liked to stop and sniff. I'd just found a spot to set another trap.

The Bear Valley wolves were known for wanderlust. They moved through the wilderness, covering great distances until they killed an elk. They liked the valley, but didn't stay if there was no food. They always seemed to return though, thus the pack's name. At this time of year, the pups were old enough to follow along. I wondered if this was the reason they were present one night and seemingly gone the next.

Day two was the charm. The trap near the gopher mound was gone, but there was no sign of which direction the animal had gone. Where was the drag mark? The brush would be disturbed if an animal were hiding there. I shaded my eyes from the sun, which had just broken over the horizon. What in the hell? I walked in wide semi-circles feeling my gut start to knot. Maybe I got a wolf and it took off cross country. I hadn't toggled my trap to something heavy like a big limb, so a wolf could have run off wearing the trap and put on a lot of distance in the sagebrush and short grass. This could get complicated in a hurry. After about 20 minutes of searching, I thought about asking the bow hunters for help.

The sun was getting higher. Not good. I would like to have been done with the wolf by now and headed out of the area. When temperatures go up, it's hard to keep a wolf's body temperature where it belongs at around 101-102 degrees. The longer a wolf is trapped, the more stressed it becomes. I wondered about running into hunters, or having them find the wolf before I did. I scanned the area once again. Nothing. Then up ahead, I noticed sunrays streaming through the pines. It looked weird. I could see each distinct sunray because of a cloud of dust rising from the edge of the trees. There was my catch. Maybe it was a badger.

As I got nearer, I could see something black digging furiously. Maybe a bear? I was pretty sure the Bear Valley wolf pack was all gray. I got closer. A black wolf. Its head was down, with one front paw digging while the other was held useless in the trap. The trap drag was hooked tight on a lone sapling. The wolf had no idea I was there.

Most wolves just lie down and hide in the nearest thicket when they're caught. Sometimes I have to listen for the jangling of the trap chain as they move around because they hear me coming. This one was crazy. I knelt quietly and removed a vial of powdered sedative, Telazol, from my pack, added sterile water with a syringe and shook it quickly. I pulled 200 milligrams into a hypodermic and filled the syringe on the end of my jab stick. Once the wolf saw me, it panicked and thrashed in wide circles. I moved in slowly from one side and it moved away from me. With each circle, I forced it to wrap the trap chain ever shorter around the sapling. When the wolf ran out of chain and showed its backside, I pushed the needle into its hip and stepped away. While I waited, I checked the radio collar to make sure the frequency written on the inside of the collar matched what I picked up on my receiver.

I had to work fast because the Telazol was only good for about an hour, sometimes less if the wolf's metabolism is up. This one was definitely up. I lifted him – a subadult male – by the scruff of his neck and farther down on his back and walked him in circles to get him untangled from the tree. Then I freed his trapped foot. My spring scale showed he weighed about 80 pounds. I laid him on my jacket and stuck a thermometer in his butt. His temperature was my biggest concern, but miraculously it was near normal.

I put a dab of ointment in each of his bright gold eyes and covered them with a bandana. Telazol keeps an animal from being able to blink or close its eyes. I put ear tags on him, fitted his radio collar, and was finishing up right about the time he was trying to get to his feet. I snapped a few photos, pulled my jacket from under him, reclaimed my bandana and walked a distance away where I kept an eye on him while he regained his senses. He eventually stumbled off, walking like a drunk. I still had six traps to check.

I wondered whether the black wolf was just a visitor, passing through. It was a big place. I walked by the rest of my traps, snapping them with the end of my trap hammer as I went. They were all empty. I coiled them, hooked them together and headed back to my truck. Before I started the engine, I pulled out my radio receiver and antennae to see where the black wolf had gone. Perhaps not surprisingly, he had traveled north and east, away from the last location of the Bear Valley pack.

I was headed back to pack my things at the cabin when I saw antlerless elk running toward the bow hunters' camp. About a hundred yards behind them came a big bull elk. When they approached a pine thicket, the bull began scraping his head on the low branches while the others stood quietly inside the tree line.

I tried to sneak by the hunters' camp, but I saw they were standing around with their coffee cups again, and they waved. I pulled in and rolled down my window – the usual drill.

"So how's the wolf trapping going? How many days are you going to try to catch one?" The ringleader was like an old buddy now. I still didn't know their names, and they never asked mine.

"I'm done and going home," I said. I tried not to betray my satisfaction.

"Why you quittin'?"

"I collared a wolf this morning. A black one. About a quarter mile from here."

The bunch looked at me, their fingers hooked in their cups.

"Are you serious?" the hunter asked.

"Yup."

"You're full of shit."

My cheap point-and-shoot camera was on the seat.

"I hope these turned out," I said, fiddling with the buttons. I handed him the camera.

There was a lot of murmuring and good-natured cursing as the guys passed the camera around. I got out and pointed to the area where I caught the wolf. It wasn't a 10-minute walk from here, I told them.

We talked a little more and I climbed back in my truck. I liked these guys. They were curious and asked questions. I didn't know what they said when I wasn't there, but I didn't really care. I liked them well enough that I did something no hunter does: tell them where the elk are.

"Hey, you fellas might ought to get your gear," I said. "There's a big bull just up in the meadow when I came by."

We shook hands one last time, and as I drove away, I could see in my rearview mirror the flurry of a bunch of hunters who had somewhere to be.

B-300

In the fall of 2011, a gray wolf from northeastern Oregon headed south. There was nothing special about this animal. It was just a wolf.

Biologists noted, by the locations beamed back from the wolf's satellite collar, that it wasn't just meandering in the range of a wolf's usual territory. It was traveling, skimming hills and valleys, staying out of sight. The wolf crossed pastures, creeks and roads, its feet moving fast. A camera hidden in the woods by a deer hunter accidentally captured a black-and-white photo of the wolf. It was stopped amid downed timber, sniffing the ground. It was looking for something.

Before long, the wolf, known to researchers as OR-7, crossed dark mountains to the south and trotted into California. It was the first wolf known to put a paw in the Golden State in nearly a century. Ranchers got tense. The wolf would start killing everything, some were certain.

Soon everyone had heard about OR-7, and a wolf doing what it does became headlines. OR-7 traveled more than 2,000 miles, searching in vain for a mate. A different wolf had tried the long-distance search nearly ten years earlier. B-45, a runty little female, swam the Snake River and traveled to the John Day area of Oregon, eating elk and minding her own business. Federal trappers flipped out, worrying that an endangered species was going to screw up their coyote-killing routine, forcing them to pick up traps and poison to keep from accidentally killing B-45. The U.S. Fish and Wildlife Service bowed to pressure from Oregon ranchers, sending in a helicopter to capture B-45 and take her back to Idaho.

But things were different now because B-45 had made it so. Her presence caused a social and bureaucratic uproar, and Oregon officials realized they had better get their act together: Wolves were coming. If not for the B-45 incident, wildlife advocates might not have noticed that agriculture interests, even in a mostly blue state like Oregon, still dictated the lives and deaths of predators. Once they became aware of this fact, wolf fans were determined to change it. By the time OR-7 went on his walkabout, they were ready. Mostly.

For a while, OR-7 was in the news almost daily. Jack Ohman, then the editorial cartoonist for The Oregonian newspaper, admired the wolf's wanderlust and started including little OR-7 drawings here and there in his cartoons, even if the wolf had nothing to do with that edition's topic. In 2012, Ohman took it a step further, declaring an OR-7 presidential campaign. The newspaper sold hundreds of bumper stickers, buttons and posters, and the wolf garnered hundreds of write-in votes for all kinds of offices. Meanwhile, an environmental group held a contest to name the wolf. The winner was "Journey," but it never caught on. OR-7 stuck. The topic of OR-7 – and the fascination with wolves, in general – rankled many in more rural eastern Oregon, who didn't think Ohman's campaign was funny or cute. They spewed criticism, acting like the wolf was the closest thing to the spawn of Satan. The pro- and anti-wolf sentiments became equally silly, reflecting, among other things, the absurd relationship between people and wolves. Some on the west side of the state were voting for a cartoon wolf wearing a coat and tie. On the east side, many believed that wolves were stalking kids at school bus stops, an idea that had been popular for years in Idaho, Wyoming and Montana. Everyone seemed to have gone nuts.

(Copyright © Oregonian Publishing Co. Reprinted with permission.)

I'd always found the best entertainment in stories conjured by the anti-wolf groups. They never exactly come out and say it, but they are afraid for their lives. They continue to worry that these reintroduced wolves will kill all of the elk, then come for us. Never mind that elk and deer numbers are at an all-time high in some areas. They believe that these transplanted Canadian wolves are different from American wolves, even though DNA tests show they are all the same. My favorite claim from anti-wolf groups is that we will all die after becoming infected by echinococcus granulosus, a kind of tapeworm that wolves carry.

If you walk into a rural grocery store in a Western state where there are wolves, you're likely to see posters with a gross color photo of what looks like a giant zit. That's the liver cyst caused by the tapeworm, they say. Wolf haters would have you believe that simply breathing the air in the woods or merrily picking berries where wolves have crapped will result in infection and death. Of course it's hogwash, but it makes for a great story. The truth is that this tapeworm also is carried by many domestic dogs as well as deer, elk and domestic sheep. Humans so rarely contract this particular tapeworm that it doesn't even register with the Centers for Disease Control. Conceivably, if you eat a lot of wolf shit – can't say that I do – you might be asking for it. I've been tested for it, and the results were negative. If I don't have this tapeworm, nobody does, because I'm certain I've handled more wolf shit than almost anyone except perhaps Dr. Doug Smith in Yellowstone National Park. Sometimes I even use gloves.

OR-7 was a star worldwide, thanks to the Internet, and this made Oregon biologists cringe. They didn't care to deal with the hoopla, and hoped the wolf didn't end up poisoned, shot or hit by a car. They answered hundreds of phone calls from people wanting to know more. OR-7 wasn't just a wolf any more; he was a survivor, a wanderer, a metaphor for us, apparently.

The public was only able to follow OR-7's story because Oregon Department of Fish and Wildlife biologists Russ Morgan and Roblyn Brown had collared him in eastern Oregon. They monitored him by satellite and a computer link as part of the Imnaha pack, one of the first wolf packs in Oregon's recent history. The biologists were under tremendous pressure from ranchers to keep track of this pack, and they did.

The sassy matriarch of OR-7's original pack in Idaho also had a collar, and had done quite a bit of traveling herself. Perhaps that wolf – B-300 – had passed her wanderlust on to her pup.

I met B-300 in the summer of 2006. It was hot and dry in Idaho, and I banged around in a state truck, looking for wolves to collar. I couldn't imagine just sitting around or playing golf in retirement. I wanted to keep doing what I did best for as long as I could. My knees weren't what they used to be, but I could find wolves, and I figured I had a lot of good years left as a field biologist. The summer turned out to be among my last working for the agency. I wasn't very good about keeping my mouth shut when it came to the way the state managed wolves. They'd killed too many, and didn't seem concerned that throngs of Idahoans and people who visited the state wanted to see this newly recovered animal conserved. I'd found it refreshing to say what I felt. I was retired. What did I care if the state fired me? Reporters who knew me from my days as a fed called me whenever things with wolves went south, which was a lot. My comments landed on the front page and the evening news. As a result, I wasn't quite fired; I just wasn't invited back again.

B-300 recovers from being re-collared in Oregon.
(Photo courtesy Oregon Department of Fish and Wildlife)

I needed to do whatever I could to make sure wolves got a fair shake, and I couldn't do it unless I was involved, so that summer I packed my truck and said goodbye to my nearly new wife. She looked kind of downcast at being left for an indefinite period. But this was my thing, and almost nothing stopped me. Come to think of it, nothing got in my way. It was probably the reason that over the years so many of us wolf biologists ended up divorced and living alone, with a bowl, a spoon and an old mattress on the floor. We were married to our jobs, and our mates finally got the picture. It had happened to me once, and I hoped it didn't happen again.

I headed north and east of Boise into the national forest, which begins almost before the last subdivision is in your rearview mirror. It doesn't take long to escape the cities in Idaho. There are a lot more wide-open places than developed ones. I'm talking about real wilderness, not parks with bicycle paths and picnic tables. Idaho has the kind of backcountry that will kill you if you're not careful. Nature bats last, as they say.

A couple of days into it, I'd already found plenty of evidence that wolves were around. It wasn't too surprising; they had done a good job of spreading themselves almost the entire width and length of the state in the ten years since reintroduction. The hills were almost empty of people this week, and the fine dust in the roads was perfect for tracking. This summer, state wildlife managers wanted their crews doing pup counts. That meant finding rendezvous sites and sneaking in on them. Fun, anyway you cut it.

But it seemed that when something was fun, it was always cut short. I rounded a corner on a mountainside and my cell phone beeped. I had a message. It was my supervisor.

"How'd you like to do some show and tell?" Steve Nadeau said. I got the feeling it wasn't a question.

The Idaho governor's office had been promised a field trip and I was the guide. It was for the Office of Species Conservation, a special department created to do battle with the feds over endangered species policy and enforcement. Its power usurped that of the state fish and game agency.

"You find some wolves," Nadeau said. "I'll bring my camper and cook for everybody."

It turned out better than I figured. The director of OSC was Jim Caswell, a 32-year veteran of the U.S. Forest Service, a tall, bespectacled bureaucrat who was a hell of a nice guy. I'd known him from my years as the federal wolf manager. His policy advisor, Jeff Allen, came along, too. I'd always enjoyed their company and I was looking forward to a little time in the field with them. I usually only ran into these guys when neckties were involved. They brought with them Calli Daly, natural resource advisor to then-U.S. Sen. Larry Craig. I hoped I could produce a wolf for them.

My wife, Jenny, made the trip over after I called and told her what was happening. I needed another pair of eyes and ears, and she was observant when it came to zeroing in on wolves. She'd signed up as my volunteer so she could ride with me whenever the mood struck her. We headed toward Lowman, a spot that was dependable for wolves. There were a bunch of small fires burning in the hills surrounding the town. Nothing abnormal about that this time of year. We'd hiked for about a half-mile on a steep trail. It was early afternoon and there was a weird rumbling in the distance, like far-off thunder that wouldn't quit. Maybe it was building up to an afternoon thunderstorm. The wind had picked up. Ahead of us, out of the cool, dark pines, was a stand of bleached tree skeletons. The ground was white, former branches turned to ash. It looked like the fire was just here, although nothing smoldered. The tree trunks swayed slightly in the hot air. There was that rumbling sound again.

"Let's get out of here."

I said it at the same time that Jenny said it. She'd stopped behind me, staring at the burn. Suddenly, we both realized the danger: We were in the eye of it, more or less – a new wildfire. We couldn't see it but it was shifting somewhere to our immediate west. It wasn't as obvious as you might think. You imagine that you could see a fire if it was in front of you. But these fires did their work in pieces, sneaking in and out of the forest, cutting you off from the place you came. Before we could turn on our heels, the wind died. It was quiet. We broke into a jog back down the trail. At the truck, delicate black ash fell through the forest openings, landing on our heads. A scribbled note was tucked under my windshield wiper:

Evacuate now! Extreme wildfire danger!

We wondered why the forest road wasn't closed, and whether other people were up there, caught unaware. We never found out. On the drive out, we passed a fire crew setting up roadblocks.

Our plans for Lowman spoiled, we headed back toward the Idaho City area. I phoned Steve to tell him about the change of plans. We'd instead be searching for the Timberline wolf pack. They might need another collar anyway. Their territory had stayed more or less in the same place – about 11 miles north of Idaho City, in steep timbered country. I'd put a collar in the pack in 2003. Suzanne Stone of Defenders of Wildlife had lobbied me then to name the pack after Timberline High School in Boise, whose mascot was, of course, the wolf.

Jenny and I set up camp ahead of everyone else in a place near Edna Creek that we'd named Nadeau Meadow because it rhymed. Besides, it's always nice to name something after the boss. We'd camped there with him earlier in the summer and it was a good place to set up: flat, wide, near a creek, and an easy place to turn a truck around.

The next day, everyone assembled and we split up to look for signs that wolves might be nearby. Check the inside curve of the road, I suggested. Wolves like to cut corners. Wolf tracks are good; wolf shit is better. Look for butterflies in the road, I said. They love wolf shit. We'd meet back at camp for lunch.

A few of the searchers came upon three dead buck sheep near a set of corrals in the woods. Despite its status as a national forest, this was also a federal grazing area. I didn't like the sound of things and followed the others to investigate. The carcasses were pretty rotten and stinky, and too decayed to tell how they died. It wouldn't surprise me to learn they were reported as wolf kills, simply because wolves were around. The bucks probably had been hauled there to breed with the ewes and may have died from causes other than predation. Most of the time it's something much less exciting that takes them – harsh weather, disease, poison plants, or a stressful journey in a crowded truck being the top candidates. When it comes to sheep, everything under the sun is waiting to tip one over. Still, the Timberline wolf pack had visited the carcasses. Their tracks gave them away.

I backtracked the wolves from the corrals northward. They were coming off a nearby ridge, following a well established sheep trail that cut through scattered sagebrush and lodgepole timber directly to the corrals. I figured that for a one-night wolf-trapping demonstration, we couldn't have found a better situation.

We parked our trucks on a road about a quarter mile above the corrals. I asked everyone to stay inside while I set wolf traps so that we didn't leave human scent unnecessarily. Before I packed my gear down the slope a hundred yards, I asked Calli if she wanted to walk with me and carry my wolf bait bucket. She had traveled all the way from Washington D.C., so I wanted her to be entertained.

Calli is petite, and I am pretty tall, but I tried to take smaller strides and asked her to stay behind me, step in my exact tracks, and try to avoid brushing against plants. I set four traps and cabled each of them to small downed aspen trees that seemed to be lying all over the place. Cabling the drag to the downed trees usually prevents a wolf from running long distances with a trap on its foot. Calli was a good sport, holding the putrid contents of the bucket for the better part of an hour while I went about my trap-setting routine. She never complained. In fact, she asked to sniff some of the lure up close. I handed her the slim twig I'd been using to gingerly dig the stuff out of its little jar. She held it as close to her nose as she dared, then shuddered.

If the wolves were around, I was certain we'd have one by morning. Darkness fell on our camp and we dug into heaping plates of chow. Then the booze came out. It was a good night.

At 6 a.m., we pulled away from camp in two trucks, though one or two in our party weren't feeling so great.

Almost as soon as we neared the trap site, I saw a drag mark, long and deep across the dusty road. We had something, and it had taken the trap with it. I got out and examined it, then motioned to the others.

"It's headed up country," I said. There were large canine tracks, too. I asked Steve and Jeff to follow the drag trail while I checked the other traps.

Nothing seemed disturbed until I got to the last trap. It was missing. Drag marks indicated this animal ran the other way, downhill toward the corrals, dragging the aspen branch behind it. A hundred yards away, I could see a big gray wolf struggling in the trees.

"Bring the truck around and meet me on the lower road," I yelled. The wolf was closer to that road than the one I'd come from. I took off running and when the wolf saw me closing the distance, it managed to turn and run, cross an open meadow and the next ribbon of road, and then plunge into thick willows along the creek bottom. I could see the bushes shaking. Now it was stuck.

Jim eased up to me in my truck, leaving Jeff and Steve with the other trapped wolf. Jenny and Calli were in the back of the pickup. I grabbed my catchpole out of the back and loaded a syringe with Telazol. I put the syringe in my breast pocket and stepped quietly toward the willows. Somewhere in there was the wolf. Or so I thought.

We heard trap chain rattling away from us. The wolf had emerged and jumped into the creek, and was now tangled up on the other side. The four of us ran to the stream bank. Jenny and I jumped in and waded across knee-deep, hoping to catch the wolf before it broke free and decided to take off across the next meadow.

"Don't get bit," I warned my wife. We were on either side of him. "Let me get this on him. You think you can hold him down?"

Jenny nodded and rattled the bushes so that the wolf would focus on her. It gave me the chance I needed to slip the noose of the catchpole over its neck and cinch it – just tight enough to keep his head away from us. I pointed the business end of the pole into the ground and the wolf went with it, a little unwillingly. I held it firm until Jenny took over. Then I took the syringe out of my pocket and pushed it into the wolf's hip. In about 10 minutes, the wolf was limp. I looked it over and saw that it was a he. Then I stepped on the trap springs and freed him. Even after all that running with the trap, his foot appeared uninjured.

He was a heavy one and I needed help carrying him across the creek. By then, Jim and Jeff appeared next to me and the three of us lifted the wolf. Jenny ran back to the truck, grabbed the camera and began snapping photos of our guests. We put the wolf on a spring scale and he came in at 105 pounds. He was about two years old. We worked fast to measure, ear tag, and collar him as B-299. We had to hurry, so we moved him to the shade of the trees to recover. I put Calli in charge of watching the wolf until he woke up.

"Holler if he wanders toward the water," I said.

We had to go. Up the hill, we had another catch.

*Jim Caswell (far left) and Jeff Allen
help me carry a Timberline pack wolf.
(Photo by Jenny Niemeyer)*

This one wasn't going to be so easy. I assumed the two were related, but this one was frantic. This was OR-7's mother, B-300, as we later tagged her. She was caught around a tree stump on a sunny hillside and she whipped and flung herself in every direction, trying to be free of the trap. She was a warrior. Later, when I learned she'd traveled a great distance, I wasn't too surprised. But right now, I was worried she'd hurt herself before I could get a sedative in her. The men surrounded her, slowly, trying to distract her enough that I could use my catchpole.

She was considerably smaller than the first wolf, but she put up a hell of a dust cloud fighting us. By the time I got an injection of Telazol in her, she had a bloody mouth from biting at everything, and was covered in dirt. So were we. Her trapped foot seemed in better shape than the rest of her. The trap chain was wound so tightly around the tree that it took a few minutes to untangle. She weighed 80 pounds and was about the same age as B-299.

Her temperature was high from all the struggling, and the day was starting to warm. After I got a collar on her, we wet her down to cool her and moved her downhill to a patch of long grass in the shadow created by two steep hills. Jenny stayed near her, watching from a short distance, to make sure she recovered and walked away.

The two wolves remained in the Timberline pack territory, and after exchanging photos and recalling the fast action of the day, we all moved on with work and life. I saw Jim at a political function a few months after the capture and he produced a handkerchief from his pocket.

"See these?" He pointed proudly at dark splotches of dried blood. "This is from that wolf."

I'd forgotten that he had offered his handkerchief to shield B-299's eyes from the sun while the wolf was drugged, and B-300 later bled a little on his hanky. He was proud of that day, and he carried the splotched cloth with him everywhere. He would never wash it, he said.

In January 2008, my phone rang. It was Russ Morgan, the wolf manager for the Oregon Department of Fish and Wildlife.

"One of your wolves is over here," he said.

Russ had been on his first flight to look for wolves that had been reported here and there in eastern Oregon. Armed with a list of radio-collar frequencies of Idaho wolves that had gone missing, he heard a signal off one side of the plane and checked. It was B-300. It wasn't until a week later that he caught sight of her. He pulled out his video camera. She was loping through the Wallowa-Whitman National Forest near the Eagle Cap Wilderness, between Medical Springs and Wallowa. She was 150 miles from where we'd collared her in Idaho. On one hand, it wasn't odd that a wolf would travel that distance. They do it all the time. Still, I wondered if she was reacting to being captured and collared. Maybe. Maybe not. The Timberline wolves were not known for wandering to far-off lands, but she'd been awfully angry about our interference in her life.

When Russ recaptured B-300 a year later, she was still in Wallowa country. He removed her defunct Idaho collar and replaced it with one owned by the State of Oregon. She became OR-2. Wolf advocates across Oregon started calling her Sophie, and by spring 2009, she had produced two litters of pups. Among the squirming pups in her second litter was OR-7. The feisty little wolf that decided Oregon was better than Idaho didn't know it, but she became the mother of the Imnaha pack in Oregon, only the second identified pack in more than 60 years.

In the fall of 2013, B-300's collar transmitted a signal for the last time. She is out there somewhere, but will probably never be found. There was talk that her disappearance coincided with the fall elk season in eastern Oregon. Maybe she'd been shot illegally. But that was just talk. A dead wolf in that part of the state would have been bragging rights for someone, but none of the state biologists heard a thing about it. Maybe the battery in her collar was the only thing that died. By 2013, she was probably about nine years old, really old for a wild wolf. Still, I wanted to think she was out there on some remote mountain. After all she'd been through, it only seemed right that she should still be on the move.

B-300's son, OR-7, backtracked several times in his seemingly endless search for – what else? A mate. He crossed the Oregon-California border six times, avoiding highways, ranches and trouble in general. He finally found a female wolf in an unexpected place: Oregon's southern Cascade Range in the Rogue River watershed. It was unexpected because no one knew she was there. She had no tracking collar, but she had navigated the backcountry, also avoiding humans while presumably looking for love, just like OR-7. In 2014, the pair had three pups and biologists declared them a pack – the first official pack in western Oregon's modern history. The Rogue pack.

Fear and Hope

An Outdoor Life magazine cover illustration from 2007 shows a man in the light of a campfire swinging a stick, beating back a pack of wolves. The animals are snarling and lunging and have blood on their muzzles. The fellow looks terrified. The cover was prompted by a real story out of northern Idaho where two men went to an area known to have wolves. One man turned his hounds loose to train them to hunt black bears and the wolves attacked his dogs, killing one and injuring others. The wolves were protecting their rendezvous site and pups. It wasn't the first time wolves had attacked dogs in the Northwest, and while the story about the dogs was believable, the insinuation that the men were next on the menu wasn't.

There are similar reports of wolves attacking hunters on horseback, and the riders bailing out of their saddles, guns blazing, trying to save their mounts. Others say they barely made it out of the woods alive, or had to build bonfires and stay up all night to protect their horses, while wolves howled all around them. There's no proof of any of this, other than the word of the victims. But their fear is real. When I hear about these incidents,

I pick up the phone and call biologists and law enforcement officers who might have been involved. They don't have much to go on either. The professionals pretty much agree that it is critical to document negative interactions between humans and wolves – if they can find them. Most of the time the reports are groundless, but they sure make for a good story.

Something a little closer to reality is the case of a north Idaho woman who was reportedly attacked by a wolf that came straight at her while she was elk hunting. She shot it. The local paper wrote it up as a wolf attack. I read the story and noted that she was cow-calling elk, wearing camouflage and, perhaps, wearing special scent to get a bull elk to come close by imitating the sound and smell of a female elk. That way she could get a better shot. There's nothing unusual about a wolf being tricked into an easy meal and instead running straight into a hunter. I've met hunters who say this has happened, but they simply stood up, waving their arms and yelling, and the wolf fled.

Aggressive wolves in the wild are rare. I suppose it's just human nature to believe that every twig that snaps in the forest is something coming to eat us. Maybe if wolves were silent creatures, we wouldn't fear them so much. People often refer to the howling, and how creepy it sounds, but I think it's the experience of a lifetime, every time I hear it. I've worked with wolves for 30 years – crawling into their dens, invading their rendezvous sites, catching them in traps where they're agitated, pinning them to the ground when they are fire-eyed and understandably pissed at me. We've looked in each other's eyes. They've growled some pretty deep, threatening growls at me. But I have yet to experience wolf aggression the way the weekend warriors do. They spend a night in the woods and come back breathless, saying wolves tried to kill them and eat all their groceries. No other animal generates this kind of storytelling, even though bears, mountain lions and even elk and deer (via car strikes) kill many more people annually than wolves ever will.

The moon rises over my camp in the Idaho mountains.
(Photo by Carter Niemeyer)

An outbreak of hysteria swept over the hamlet of Garden Valley, Idaho, in 2003, when a woman discovered a single wolf print in the snow on her deck. It was a Sunday, but I drove up there because that's what I did. I was never unavailable. When I got there, I discovered I was the focus of a town meeting, held at a local bar, where I was berated and cursed, especially by a fellow who announced that he was just a working man, a truck driver, who didn't think he should have to put up with wolves in his rural mountain town.

"I'll be glad to go home, folks. You're the ones who called me," I said over the din, looking straight at the trucker. "I can tell you I have better things to do on a Sunday."

An elderly woman stood and told everyone to shut up.

When we finally got past the hysterics and went to look at the track, it had almost become an afterthought. Though it was late afternoon, the snow hadn't budged. Someone had put a coffee can over the single track. When I called it a dog print, the small crowd that had followed me burst into argument again.

"Look," I said, pulling a softball-sized plaster wolf track out of my pack and plunking it down next to the snowy dog print. It had come in handy many times over the years. "This is a wolf track."

The crowd quieted.

"Hey, cool! Where can I get one of those?" A woman poked her head through the circle of onlookers.

The excitement was over, and the people wandered away, murmuring. I had ruined it for them. The truck driver who was so angry earlier approached me as I zipped my wolf track into its plastic bag.

"Hey, stop by sometime for a game of cribbage!" he winked.

Wolves were few and far between when I moved to Montana in 1973. They were a rumor, really, killed off long before I arrived on the scene by the same federal government that put them back in the 1990s. There was no room for this animal in the Old West. Sometimes I think there's no room for it in the new West, even with all the ways we think we have improved.

One of the many things I have learned is this: Scientists and advocates can write reports until their fingers fall off trying to persuade people otherwise, but the basic nature of humans is that they fear wolves. They also distrust their government. Put the two together and it's a powder keg. But we can overcome fear. I have met many people with good heads and good hearts, and I believe they want to learn about wolves in order to help dispel the myths that surround these animals. I'm also confident that the American public would never condone another national wolf eradication program. We're not those people anymore. At least I hope we're not.

Wolves have killed only two people in the last 100 years in North America: a woman in Alaska who was jogging along a remote road, and a man who was hiking in Saskatchewan. (A bear might have been killed him. The coroner wasn't sure.) There are so few deaths attributed to wolves that the numbers barely register with state or federal agencies or health departments. Contrast that with bear attacks, or even dog attacks. The fear that wolves engender is largely unwarranted, but it is living proof that our imaginations know no bounds.

Science shows us that wolves do the land good, although much of it isn't completely understood. Lots of very smart people – mostly state or federal wildlife agencies and graduate students – produce reams of documents detailing their scientific findings about wolves. We know that their social structure is, ironically, much like ours. They are family-oriented, even tribal in their affiliations, and don't always take kindly to strangers, sometimes opting to kill outsider wolves (and risk being killed) rather than be overrun by new blood. On occasion, all of this is turned on its head, and a pack accepts a lone wolf, but that is the nature of the wild. It is not always predictable, and we don't always understand it. For the most part, wolves run away rather than fight. Fighting carries a lot of risk.

Being hunters, wolves are natural-born optimists. They go after prey, expecting to kill it. But they also are opportunists, eating whatever is easiest and most available. They seem to weigh their options, deciding whether the benefits of chasing an animal three or four times their size outweighs the risk. After all, there is a real possibility they will be kicked in the head or skewered with an antler, or stared down by an ornery range cow that refuses to run. I've seen plenty of wolves hobbling around, living their lives after an injury. Wolves don't always win. Often they are outrun, injured in the pursuit, or foiled when the intended meal jumps into a deep river and crosses to the other side. The wolves might follow, but in the time it would take to cross, fighting the current, they've lost the edge, and thus the battle. Sometimes all wolves can come up with for supper is a ground squirrel. They prefer to kill their prey on the run, and elk and deer can run damn fast because they and the wolves evolved together. A wolf pack needs to travel far and wide because its prey does, and the prey always regulates the predator. That is a fact. When the prey is abundant, the predators thrive, and when the prey struggles, wolves, bears and lions die, too.

It is also a fact that nutrition and food availability rather than predator pressure determine whether elk and deer populations climb or fall. Killing predators in the haphazard ways we allow – trophy hunting and general pack destruction to stop livestock killings – creates chaos on the landscape, often leading to more livestock depredations as inexperienced wolves from other broken families fill the void. A pack of wolves living around livestock and not killing those animals is functioning like a pack of guard dogs. They are preserving their territory. If you remove those wolves just because they might kill livestock, they may be replaced with another pack that's not so friendly.

We have all heard that predators make their prey stronger by whittling away at the weak. But whether they help with other, more mysterious things like aspen re-growth and stream characteristics remains unclear. Professors William Ripple and Robert Beschta at Oregon State University wondered why aspen and cottonwood trees had stopped growing in Yellowstone National Park, and set out with their measuring sticks and tree core-testers to figure it out. They discovered that in the mid-1920s, around the time of the killing of the last wolf in the park, the trees stopped growing. Their core samples told them there were few trees younger than 70 years old. Ripple and Beschta posited that once wolves were gone, the elk quickly became overabundant and lost fear, lingering in stream bottoms and eating every last delicious sapling to the ground. As a result of this lingering, the stream banks eroded and widened, particularly in the savanna-like Lamar Valley. The water warmed and became muddy. The beaver that once lived there had no food and no shelter, so they disappeared, and with them the small pools they had created by building dams, which in turn had provided quiet waters for willow growth. The willows were needed to shade and cool the river for prized Yellowstone trout and other fish, as well as songbirds and insects. The professors' hypothesis was that the simple removal of wolves caused an eco-system crash, a decades-old theory known in scientific circles as "trophic cascades." It appears that putting the wolves back has forced elk back into a natural frame of mind: watchful. They quit hanging around like cattle in the stream bottoms, and so began the recovery of plants associated with streams and rivers. That is why wolves and other large predators are called "keystone" species. Without them, the system is not whole.

The theory was highly praised at first, and then criticized, but no one yet has come up with a more plausible explanation for the ecosystem revival that started once the wolves came back to Yellowstone. The same sort of study could take place in remote Bear Valley, Idaho, a land recently free of livestock, and the home of wolves and elk and wilderness itself.

Wildlife studies are not an exact science. It's likely that the aspens are growing again in Yellowstone because wolves push the elk around and keep them from munching away at the new aspen growth. But even if that's not the sole reason, it's probably part of the reason. Whether it is or isn't, shouldn't we stop and think about these things, and consider that our actions can have a huge and lasting effect on wild creatures and wild places? Letting things be is the hardest thing for people. From the start, Ed Bangs of the U.S. Fish and Wildlife Service nailed it: "The best habitat for the wolf lies in the human heart."

I know people who will never see a wolf because they are unable to clamber into the hills. But they tell me that knowing wolves are out there – and bears and cougars and wild, untamed places – makes them smile. It's something that comes up in American wildlife surveys over and over again: Just knowing that somewhere things are wild is enough. Others see it differently, and a wolf trotting across the hills gets lined up in their rifle sights because it doesn't belong in their version of the way things should be. They just leave it there to rot because they think they're helping balance the scales somehow, possibly thinking that fewer wolves mean more elk. Their reasoning is fundamentally flawed in a dozen ways, but they're not ruled by reason. No matter how smart and complex and technological we've become, we are creatures ruled by our emotions. Lucky for wolves, they have long legs and big feet, and can move like the wind. When the going gets tough, the wolves move out. And they keep moving.

When I started out as a trapper, I was eager, and didn't ask too many questions – even of myself. I didn't believe I needed to justify killing animals. In fact, I never thought about it at all. I just did it, the way a farmer picks corn. I was a fur trapper, killing animals for the price of their pelts. I didn't do it for jollies. Those pelts paid for my college education and my infant daughter's hospital bills when she was gravely ill, and kept a roof over my family's head. It was a natural transition to become a federal trapper, taking out "problem" skunks, coyotes, bears, you name it, because the ranchers and the management agencies that serve them said they needed killing. But killing those animals, I discovered, didn't really cure anything. The fact that we had to keep doing it in the same places every year proved it. I started thinking about this. Why don't ranchers have to do a better job of taking care of their animals so they're not attacked in the first place? Why should the government be involved in killing predators? Many of these animals are on public land. They, and the land, belong to all of us. These issues swirled in my head. Keeping the status quo wasn't a good answer. I know now that most of the predator killing I did was unjustified, especially when I did it on public land. That is holy ground to me. It took me quite a few years to gather up all of these thoughts and decide how I felt about what I did for a living, and whether it was right or wrong. I spread my actions out for a look, and I kept coming back to the same spot: At the time, trapping was everything to me. I wouldn't take back most of what I did. After all, it taught me almost everything I know about wildlife. But that doesn't mean I'm the same now.

Wolf reintroduction was talked about for years. It finally happened in the mid-1990s because all of the politics lined up perfectly. Once wolves were turned loose in the Northern Rockies, I underestimated their ability to recover their numbers. In fact, their recovery has been a breathtaking success. Later, when wolves proved not to be the problem I'd heard they could be, I underestimated people's ability to hang on to old grudges

A male gray wolf rests in the Frank Church
River of No Return Wilderness.
(Photo by Jenny Niemeyer)

and crazy ideas. Bringing back wolves gave certain people in the West a shiny new reason to argue and dig in their heels, a favorite American pastime. I went into it thinking it was just a task. But I came out on the other side realizing that this animal – the wolf – was a key feature of many people's lives. It mattered to them that the wolf was restored. For some, nothing mattered as much. The wolf represented all that is wild. In hindsight, I understand.

My experiences with wolves changed me, perhaps more than anything ever has. I met people with whom I never thought I would associate – environmentalists, wolf advocates, there were a lot of terms for them. Some of the terms weren't so nice. But I liked these people. They thought about the whole instead of the parts. They talked to everyone and gathered up all the ideas, even those they didn't like. They were hopeful. I was intrigued. I mostly hung around trappers, hunters and ranchers. Nobody I knew was willing to entertain the idea of a wolf. But I thought it sounded kind of cool. Who wouldn't want a big, beautiful native predator out there? I didn't see what the big deal was. It was returning nature to itself. I never thought of one animal or another as some kind of enemy, or some kind of god. They were just animals. Maybe I'd hunt one some day. Or maybe I'd just sit on a hill, glassing for them. I thought they all deserved to be here. I never noticed until later that the wolf huggers and I were of similar minds, even though our lives and backgrounds could not have been less alike. I may have never said it out loud, but I wanted to see more of the natural world restored. So did they. In that sense, the wolf advocates won because the wolves have returned. Now these animals must take care of themselves. They certainly are tough and resilient enough.

In the three-state recovery area of Idaho, Montana and Wyoming, we've proved that we can knock the hell out of wolves and they keep going. In fact, up to 35 percent of a wolf population can be killed without hurting the overall population. Since 1995, one wolf has been killed by the government or by sport hunting and trapping for every domestic sheep confirmed killed by wolves in the West. That's 4,300 wolves. That still leaves, at this writing, nearly 1,800 wolves and 100 breeding pairs in the three-state recovery area. Of course, that might be overstating things. Or not. The methods Idaho, Wyoming and Montana use to count wolves don't yield accurate numbers, only estimates. Yellowstone is the only place with accurate wolf counts, and their numbers have fluctuated in the past few years as wolf territories fill up and conflicts between wolves increase. Contrary to what you hear, the available habitat can only hold so many wolves. But wolves survive because that's what they do, and in order to do that they disperse to new areas – hopefully places where people will tolerate them.

The simplest ideas often are the most difficult to put into action. The wolf's survival is completely tied to social carrying capacity, or to put it more simply: How many wolves will we tolerate? It's an egocentric idea, that our tolerance of large predators has everything to do with whether they still exist on this earth, but it's a fact, and it's where the plan on the drawing board begins. Large predators everywhere face an ever-expanding number of problems, most notably habitat loss and a changing climate. Given that people would often rather fight than switch attitudes or allegiances, there may not be time to bend every mind toward tolerance. But there's time to bend some, and that's a vital beginning.

There will always be times when a few wolves here or there must be killed, and there will likely always be hunting seasons for them. These are not things that will change quickly. If done with restraint, however, these takings have no chance of affecting overall wolf populations. That's not to say it's right, or that it doesn't affect wolf families, but morality is a murky area mostly not considered by wildlife managers. Occasional killing and limited hunting don't concern me as much as the justification for these actions. Why are we doing what we do to wolves? That should always be the first question, and if the reason isn't a damn good one, then this is the area for a fight. It's a new era because wolves are here to stay. If that isn't a victory, I don't know what is.

Based on what they need to survive – food and freedom from human persecution – wolves could live in a lot of places in the United States. It will be tough going though. We have drawn a lot of lines in the sand. We've spread ourselves across the landscape and posted "KEEP OUT" signs – literally and figuratively. A creature as wild and far-traveling as the wolf has few places that it can call home. But there are some places in the West that will be a wolf's land forever. They are the steep forests and mountain meadows where people seldom go. They are mostly public lands, mysterious spots on the map that are remote and rugged and intimidating in their quietness. These places will protect the wolves. And maybe that's as good as it gets.

Roger Stradley (left) and Dr. Doug Smith prepare to fly in Yellowstone.
(Photo by Carter Niemeyer)

Acknowledgments

The act of reintroducing wolves to the Northern Rockies required amazing timing, truly remarkable people and a bottomless supply of energy and hope. I am proud to have been a part of it. Many of those same people helped me with the details of this book, and I am indebted to them: Dr. Doug Smith, Deb Guernsey, Ed Bangs, Joe Fontaine, Mike Phillips, Rick McIntyre, Rich McDonald, Dr. L. David Mech, Dr. Mark Johnson, Dr. William Ripple, Dr. Robert Beschta, Russ Morgan, Gary Brennan, Rick Williamson, Jason Husseman, Adam Gall, Todd Wilkinson and Josh Stanley.

My thanks also goes to pilot Roger Stradley, my eye-in-the-sky, who has logged tens of thousands of hours in his plane, flying Yellowstone and the surrounding vicinity helping us find wolves. Thanks also to readers Paul Regan, Tom Hallman, Jr., Oliver Starr, Rhonda Lanier and Kristi Lloyd.

In the past few years, I've lost several friends who figured prominently in the wolf world, including Tom Meier, Dave Spicer, Ron Gipe, "Big Dave" Nelson, Dick Baker, Eddie Baker and Eron Coiner. Sadly, this list grows longer every year.

My greatest appreciation goes to my wife, Jenny, who gave selflessly of her love, patience, time and energy to, first, inspire me to write another book, and second, be its primary editor. She and editor Dee Lane untangled a mountain of editorial knots so that I could tell my stories clearly, and Beth Fischer took everything and designed it into the book you now hold in your hands.

Definitions and Explanations

Carbofuran: one of the most toxic carbamate pesticides. It was first registered in the United States in 1969. It is marketed under the trade names Furadan, by FMC Corporation and is used to control insects in a wide variety of field crops, including potatoes, corn and soybeans. It is a systemic insecticide, which means that the plant absorbs it through the roots, and from here the plant distributes it throughout its organs where insecticidal concentrations are attained. Carbofuran has been illegally used to intentionally poison wildlife in the U.S., Canada and Great Britain. Poisoned wildlife include coyotes, kites, golden eagles and buzzards. Secondary fatal poisoning of domestic and wild animals has been documented, specifically, raptors (bald eagles and golden eagles), domestic dogs, raccoons, vultures and other scavengers. In Kenya, farmers sometimes use carbofuran to kill lions and other predators.

In a number of publicized incidents worldwide, carbofuran has also been used to poison domestic pets. Carbofuran has one of the highest acute toxicities to humans of any insecticide. Carbofuran is known to be particularly toxic to birds. In its granular form, a single grain will kill a bird. The U.S. Environmental Protection Agency banned carbofuran, which had been used on corn, potatoes and sunflowers, in 2009, after it was linked to water contamination and health problems suffered by farm workers.

Fladry: A line of rope, twine or heavy string mounted along the top of a fence or between portable posts from which are suspended strips of fabric or colored flags (usually red) that will flap in a breeze, intended to deter wolves from crossing the fence-line. Fladry lines have been used for this purpose for several centuries, traditionally for hunting wolves in eastern Europe, where the wolves were driven through the middle of two parallel sets of fladry toward hunters waiting on one end. It is unknown why wolves are reluctant to cross the flapping flags, or why red is most often employed. The deterrent effect is temporary, and wolves may cross under the flags if it is left up too long. An experiment in open, forested range near Salmon, Idaho, in early summer 2002, kept wolves away from cattle for 65 days. In that study, volunteers for Defenders of Wildlife strung nine miles of fladry. Other studies show that fladry can be effective for three to five months. Its use is usually limited to small pastures, however, because it requires daily monitoring to ensure it hasn't fallen down or tangled. More recently, Idaho trapper Rick Williamson added a line of portable electric fence along with fladry (he coined it "turbo-fladry) as extra protection for livestock. Fladry should be removed and stored when not in use so wolves do not become habituated to it.

Endangered Species Act (ESA): Enacted in 1973, under President Richard Nixon, the purpose of the ESA is to protect and recover imperiled species and the ecosystems upon which they depend. It is administered by the U.S. Fish and Wildlife Service (FWS) and the Commerce Department's National Marine Fisheries Service (NMFS), under the umbrella of the Secretary of the Interior. The FWS has primary responsibility for terrestrial and freshwater organisms, while the responsibilities of NMFS are mainly marine wildlife such as whales and anadromous fish such as salmon. Under the ESA, species may be listed as either endangered or threatened. "Endangered" means a species is in danger of extinction throughout all or a significant portion of its range. "Threatened" means a species is likely to become endangered within the foreseeable future. All species of plants and animals, except pest insects, are eligible for listing as endangered or threatened. For the purposes of the ESA, Congress defined species to include subspecies, varieties, and, for vertebrates (such as wolves,) distinct population segments. In order for a species to be listed, it must be determined to be imperiled due to any one of the following "five listing factors:" (1) the present or threatened destruction, modification, or curtailment of its habitat or range; (2) overutilization for commercial, recreational, scientific, or educational purposes; (3) disease or predation; (4) the inadequacy of existing regulatory mechanisms; or (5) other natural or manmade factors affecting its continued existence. In order for certain species to not only be listed in the first place, but also able to recover, certain exceptions are allowed within the law. Wolves in the three-state recovery area in the Northern Rockies were managed under Section 10(a)1(a) of the Act, which allows "take" (killing) by agencies, which would otherwise not be allowed. In other words, the killing of problem wolves bought survival of the species as a whole in the designated 3-state recovery area of central Idaho, northwest Montana and Wyoming. As published in its final environmental impact statement regarding wolf reintroduction, the FWS was not concerned with recovery of wolves outside of the 3-state recovery area, nor with keeping wolves listed once their population reached a certain point. It is the goal and stated purpose of the ESA to be a stop-gap measure to recover and delist imperiled species, not to keep them under permanent federal protection. Sometimes, however, recovery takes many years.

A Conversation with
Carter Niemeyer

What are you doing these days?

I retired from the U.S. Fish and Wildlife Service in 2006, and published my first memoir, Wolfer, in 2010. These days I still trap wolves where there's a particular need, but mostly I'm a consultant, which is what you do when you're a retired anything. Most recently I've been involved in a livestock/wolf interaction study being conducted by graduate students under the direction of Dr. Rob Wielgus, associate professor and director of the Large Carnivore Conservation Lab at Washington State University's School of the Environment. I also do a bit of consulting internationally. My wife tells me that most people have jobs that are not very exciting or interesting, and for that reason, if no other, I am obliged to share my experiences with others. I felt that I still had some stories to tell after Wolfer, so she helped me put them in Wolf Land.

Give us a capsule description of wolves.

The wolf, canis lupus, is the distant relative of domestic dogs. It is a magnificent beast designed to do one thing: kill other animals, elk and deer and other large ungulates in particular, in order to feed itself. To that end, they have slim bodies, long legs and big feet for traveling tremendous distances. To make their complex lives work, they move to new lands frequently, following game and seeking to establish new territories. They prefer to live near a constant water source such as a marsh or stream. Wolves can be gray or black or any combination of the two colors. Black and gray-colored wolves can turn white (much like people) due to old age, and research suggests that younger wolves may turn white due to injury or trauma. A pack generally has one breeding pair that mate in mid-February. Four to six pups are born in mid-April in a den that can be anything from a converted badger hole to an elaborate excavation. Some wolves give birth in the open, right under a tree.

How did you get into wolf work?

I didn't start out thinking about wolves. In fact, for half of my life I never thought about them at all. I am from rural Iowa, and wolves are not a topic of conversation there. I am, however, a trapper, and that is where life for me really began. When I was 9, my dad showed me how to catch pocket gophers and take them to the courthouse for bounty. It was the 1950s, and that's what rural kids did for fun and comic book money. But then something unexpected happened: I became good at it. I moved from pocket gophers to muskrats to foxes. Friends at the Iowa Conservation Commission, where I was briefly employed, stayed after me to go to college. I went, including graduate school, but I spent a lot of time looking out the window. I just wanted to trap. I ended up in Montana after graduate school and was in the right place at the right time when wolf reintroduction became a reality.

How big do wolves get?

If you remember that wolves spend their lives in long-distance pursuit and travel, it makes sense that they're large animals, but not huge. That would require too much energy to maintain and is not efficient. The biggest wolf I ever handled was a male weighing 141 pounds. If its stomach had been empty, it probably would have weighed 125-130 pounds. That is about as big as they get, though some are slightly larger. Female wolves are slightly smaller, ranging from 65-115 pounds. Colleagues in Alaska say that their wolves weigh the same. Fish and game records in Montana, Idaho and Wyoming show that wolves rarely exceed 125 pounds. One hundred pounds is about average. You might hear about mega-wolves that weigh 250 pounds, but there's no such thing. When wolves live in an area of abundant game animals and have all they can eat, including bison, moose, elk and deer, they can grow to their full potential. The size of a wolf is more dependent on food availability than genetics, but if the two qualities occur together, you get some mighty fine, majestic, beautiful carnivores.

What should a person do if he comes upon a wolf in the wild?

Wolves are inherently suspicious of people. They won't allow you to approach them if they can help it, and once they are aware of you, they disappear. This often happens before you are ever aware of the wolf's presence, but if you surprise each other you may only get a moment or two of being stared at before the animal turns around and runs away. Cherish it and try not to panic. If you find yourself being howled at by one or more wolves, you may be close to their den or their pups, and you probably are standing somewhere near their rendezvous site. They are expressing their dismay. Experience it, then retreat quietly, keeping your binoculars close by. You may get to see the whole pack. The chances of being attacked are extremely slim. If you are interested in returning to show others, take a GPS reading so you can find your way back.

How can people find wolves?

In states where wolves are hunted, trapped or killed regularly because they kill livestock, wolves can become very leery of people and be difficult to find, but if you have time and a full tank of gas, and the wolves are anywhere in the area, you can find signs of them. I drive remote mountain roads and look in the fine dust for wolf tracks. In summer, butterflies are a giveaway, as they often sit on wolf poop. Camp on a hilltop and give a howl at dawn and dusk. Then listen. You may hear them answer you, if they're within earshot. In areas where wolves are known to live, you may only see them in the early morning or just before dusk. Your best chance to see wolves in the wild is at Yellowstone National Park, where (especially if you have limited time) you can take advantage of the expertise of people who follow wolves in the park. They set up spotting scopes along the road, or nearby, almost daily. There is often a small crowd watching the wolves, and experts can provide interesting background on individual animals. Park employee Rick McIntyre has followed the lives of Yellowstone's wolves daily for 20 years and can almost always be found in the crowd.

I want to work with wolves. Where do I start?

They say that you should do what you love and the money will follow, but these days you need to get your ticket punched if you want to get into wildlife work. You need to go to college and possibly graduate school, and you need to do as much volunteer work as possible in your specific area of interest. Say yes to hands-on opportunities with professional wildlife organizations, even if you don't get paid very well (or at all.) Accept that in wildlife work you won't get rich, but if you want to have an adventure instead of sitting in a cubicle, field work is the way to go. Being flexible, open-minded and committed to your passion will open doors you haven't even considered, and one day the professionals will be knocking on your door instead of vice versa. This is exactly how it went for me. I had learned the intricacies of fox trapping from an Iowan named George Good because trapping was what I loved. I never thought about it coming in handy as a career, but George must have taught me well because I paid my tuition with the money I made putting up fur. Word got back to one of my professors at Iowa State University who was looking for a trapper for a rabies study. He asked me to enroll in graduate school. It was unheard of, but they needed a trapper. I did it, and because I said yes to school, I graduated with bachelor's and master's degrees in wildlife biology (with minors in chemistry and botany.) I never considered myself a student, but I did well because I loved the subject matter. That made it easy. Almost immediately afterward, I got a government job in Montana, trapping and documenting skunks that carried rabies. I climbed aboard a train and went West without thinking twice. Once I arrived in the West, I knew I would never leave. The lesson here? Follow your heart.

Would you eat wolf meat?

People have a hang-up about it, I know, but yes, if it was a matter of survival, I could eat wolf meat. It's not exactly in my search mode for food, however. I don't buy the myth that wolves would taste disgusting because they eat dead animals. Wolves just prefer theirs rare. The only concern I'd have about eating a predator would be parasites, but that's if it was undercooked. Tapeworms occur in most wildlife, so wolves are not special in that regard. I have eaten black bear and lion steaks and they were quite good. I think a wolf would be, too, but I can't picture a circumstance when I would tie a napkin around my neck and cut into one. A trapper I know in Montana once said, "I don't eat nothin' that can eat me." It's probably a good rule of thumb.

Are wolves still endangered?

With the exception of the Mexican gray wolf, the U.S. Fish and Wildlife Service (USFWS) no longer considers wolves endangered and has removed Endangered Species Act protections from wolf populations in the lower 48 states. However, litigation by conservation groups has resulted in some populations of wolves being re-listed by the courts. ndividual states may choose to protect wolves under state endangered species acts and write rules determining ways the animals will be managed. Wolf populations in Canada currently number between 50,000 and 60,000, providing a reservoir of wolves that can freely disperse into the U.S. to augment wolf numbers here. Alaska is home to 8,000-11,000 wolves.

What can I do to help protect wolves?

Protecting wolves begins with adequate laws to ensure that populations are maintained at sustainable levels, which will guarantee viability into the future. As an individual, you can stay informed about the status of wolves and stay up-to-date on potential threats to their populations. You can advocate for their protection as an individual or join conservation groups, which provide a stronger voice. It's important to speak up to state wild-life agencies if you think wolf populations are at risk.

Questions for Book Groups

1. In 1995-96, the U.S. government tried to restore the wolf population, which had been killed nearly to extinction, by gathering wolves from Canada and reintroducing them in the United States. Do you think that was a good idea? How much should government intervene to maintain a species?

2. Have you spent time in wild areas? How did it affect you?

3. If you haven't spent time in wild areas, do you agree with the idea that it's important to know that wild places exist?

4. Carter Niemeyer writes that, at first, we thought that each wolf mattered, but after we realized how prolific and resilient they were, we just killed them. Do you think individual animals matter if the species is stable? Why or why not?

5. Are you more afraid of some animals than others? How do you feel about wolves? What causes this fear and what, if anything, can be done about it?

6. Niemeyer says that ranchers who use public lands for grazing sheep or cattle should understand that it's just part of doing business when they lose some to predators. Do you agree? Should ranchers be able to use public lands at all?

7. Do you see a difference in the way people in urban and rural areas think about wildlife? If so, is it a divide that can be bridged?

8. Niemeyer confesses that his views changed over time, both from experience and exposure to people with different ideas. Is there any issue where your views have changed? What changed your mind?

9. Can wolves and humans co-exist?

10. Did you know that killing wolves is the preferred method of dealing with "problem" wolves, and that people are not required by law to do anything to aid in preventing injury or death to livestock or pets? Do you agree with this?

11. Where should wild wolves live? Why?

Suggested Reading and Resources General Interest

Barker, Rocky. 1993. *Saving All the Parts: Reconciling Economics and the Endangered Species Act.* Island Press.

Crumley, J. 2010. *The Last Wolf.* Birlinn Limited – Edinburgh.

Dutcher, J. and J. 2013. *The Hidden Life of Wolves.* National Geographic Society.

Eisenberg, C. 2014. *The Carnivore Way.* Island Press.

Endangered Species Act of 1973, as amended (16 USC 1531-1543)

Federal Animal Damage Control Act of 1931, as amended (7 USC 426-426d)

Fischer, Hank. 1995. *Wolf Wars.* Falcon Press.

Hayes, B. 2010. *Wolves of the Yukon.* Published by Bob Hayes. Whitehorse, Yukon Territory, Canada.

Living With Wolves - www.livingwithwolves.org

McIntyre, R. 1995. *War Against the Wolf: America's Campaign to Exterminate the Wolf.* Stillwater, Minnesota: Voyageur Press.

McNamee, T. 1997. *The Return of the Wolf to Yellowstone.* Henry Holt and Company – New York.

McNamee, T. 2014. *The Killing of Wolf Number Ten.* Prospecta Press.

Nash, Roderick. 1967. *Wilderness and the American Mind.* (Revised/reprinted 1973) Yale University.

Robinson, Michael, J. 2005. *Predatory Bureaucracy: The Extermination of Wolves and the Transformation of the West.* University Press of Colorado.

Smith, D., and G. Ferguson. 2005. *Decade of the Wolf: Returning the Wild to Yellowstone.* The Lyons Press, Guilford, Connecticut.

The Wildlife News - www.thewildlifenews.com

Van Tighem, K. 2013. *The Homeward Wolf.* Rocky Mountain Books.

Suggested Reading and Resources Academic

Bradley, E.H. 2004. *An evaluation of wolf-livestock conflicts and management in the northwestern United States.* M.S. thesis, University of Montana. Missoula, MT. 83 pp.

Bradley, E.H., H.S. Robinson, E.E. Bangs, K. Kunkel, M.D. Jimenez, J.A. Gude, and T. Grimm. 2015. *Effects of wolf removal on livestock depredation recurrence and wolf recovery in Montana, Idaho, and Wyoming.* Journal of Wildlife Management 79: in press. (December 2015)

Carbyn, L.N., S.H. Fritts, and D.R. Seip. 1995. *Ecology and Conservation of Wolves in a Changing World.* Canadian Circumpolar Institute, Occasional Publication No. 35, 642 pp.

Haber, G., and M.B. Holleman. 2013. *Among Wolves.* University of Alaska Press. 284 pp.

Heberlein, T.A. 2012. *Navigating Environment Attitudes.* Oxford University Press. 228 pp.

King, C.L. 1965. *Reasons for the Decline of Game in the Big Horn Basin of Wyoming (Illustrated with Photographs).* Vantage Press. New York. 161 pp.

McNay, M.E. 2002. *A case history of wolf-human encounters in Alaska and Canada.* Alaska Department of Fish and Game Wildlife Technical Bulletin 13. 45 pp.

Mech, L.D. 1970. *The wolf: the ecology and behavior of an endangered species*. Doubleday/Natural History Press, Garden City, N.Y. 384 pp.

Mech, L.D. 2012. *Is Science in Danger of Sanctifying the Wolf?* Biological Conservation Vol. 150 Issue 1, pp. 143-149.

Mech, L.D., and L. Boitani. 2007. New edition. *Wolves: Behavior, Ecology and Conservation*. University of Chicago Press. 472 pp.

Mech, L.D., D.W. Smith and D.R. MacNulty. 2015. *Wolves on the Hunt: The Behavior of Wolves Hunting Wild Prey*. University of Chicago Press. 208 pp.

Oakleaf, J.K. 2002. *Wolf-cattle interactions and habitat selection by recolonizing wolves in the northwestern United States*. M.S. Thesis, University of Idaho, Moscow, Idaho. 67 pp.

Ripple, W.J., Estes, J.A., Beschta, R.L., Wilmers, C.C., Ritchie, E.G., Hebblewhite, M., Berger, J., Elmhagen, B., Letnic, M., Nelson, M.P., Schmitz, O.J., Smith, D.W., Wallach, A.D., Wirsing, A.J. 2014. *Status and Ecological Effects of the World's Largest Carnivores*. Science 343: 1241484

Shivik, J.A. 2014. *The Predator Paradox: Ending the War with Wolves, Bears, Cougars, and Coyotes*. Beacon Press. 196 pp.

Trapp, J.R. 2004. *Wolf den site selection in the Northern Rocky Mountains*. Thesis, Prescott College, Prescott, Arizona, USA. 63 pp.

United States Department of the Interior, U. S. Fish and Wildlife Service. *Final Environmental Impact Statement, The Reintroduction of Gray Wolves to Yellowstone National Park and Central Idaho*. 1994. USFWS, Helena, Montana. Available online at www.fws.gov/mountain-prairie/species/mammals/wolf/

Wielgus R.B., Peebles K.A. (2014) *Effects of Wolf Mortality on Livestock Depredations*. PLoS ONE 9(12): e113505. doi:10.1371/journal.pone.0113505

Young, S.P., and E.A. Goldman. 1944. *The Wolves of North America*. Dover, New York, N.Y./American Wildlife Institute, Washington, D.C. 636 pp.

CPSIA information can be obtained
at www.ICGtesting.com
Printed in the USA
LVOW13s1802151216
517424LV00010B/1460/P